THE NEW
BRIDE'S BOOK
OF
ETIQUETTE

THE NEW BRIDE'S BOOK
OF
ETIQUETTE

By the Editors of *Bride's* Magazine
with Susan D. Hackman

Publishers · GROSSET & DUNLAP · New York

Acknowledgments

Bride's acknowledges contributions on this *New Bride's Book of Etiquette* from staff members Christine Grillo, Susan D. Hackman, Louise Havens, Helen Johnson, Charlotte Knabel, Victoria Peslak, Christine Pattison Ranges, Margaret Marchese Rosner, and Elizabeth Thayer.

Cover photograph by Denis Piel
Back cover photograph by Barbara Bersell
Sketches by Susan Gray

Foreword

As a woman and man who have agreed to marry, you are about to embark upon one of life's richest and most rewarding adventures. No one, of course, thinks marriage is *easy* anymore. We have scores of bleak statistics to prove that failure is possible, and problems certainly probable. And yet we persist. Why?

Because marriage—reexamined, restructured, modernized, and customized—is the best (though admittedly imperfect) institution of total personal commitment. And without commitment, without the daily interaction of two dedicated personalities, most of us feel vaguely empty and unfulfilled, without distinct roots or purpose. Private agreements between loving couples are frequent and temporarily effective. Yet no tacit understanding can substitute for the joyous pride a couple can feel in pledging their love and devotion before the immediate world. And then in recognizing the responsibility to make their marriage work.

Our society, buffeted as it is by revolution and change, yearns for the security that comes from trusting in our own humanity. What better promise for the future than to "love, honor, and cherish"? What more nourishing platform for growth and development than the strength that two human beings can *give* each other—through tenderness, discipline, and will.

Of course, there is a lighter tone to this book. *The New Bride's Book of Etiquette* is about invitations and receiving lines, about photographs and receptions, about showers and gifts and going-away clothes. But it is also about feelings—those subtle courtesies and kindnesses that smooth relationships between families and friends ... and between two very *special* friends—you and your fiancé.

Read between the lines as you look up information about announcing your engagement, writing your own vows, choosing your attendants as well as the guest list. Notice how this, the Fourth Edition of the *Bride's Book of Etiquette,* with its newly revised and updated text, avoids clichés and rigid rules, depending instead upon good taste and common sense for its authority. There is a chapter specifically for those who are starting married life *again,* as well as complete information for those who have never planned a party, much less a formal wedding for two hundred guests.

Every page of this book is designed to answer your every question. Whether you're in doubt about inviting your four-year-old niece to be a flower girl, or wondering where your divorced father-in-law (to-be) should sit at the reception, depend upon us to come up with an understanding—and sensible—solution.

And know that every person who has been connected with this book (including *other* brides and grooms whose ideas have appeared in *Bride's* Magazine over the years and are incorporated in this volume) wishes you and your future husband a very special toast:

Health, happiness, and prosperity . . . and plenty of time to enjoy them!

Barbara Tober
Editor-in-Chief
Bride's

Contents

THE NEW
BRIDE'S BOOK
OF
ETIQUETTE

1
Your Engagement

Parties and plans and the delightful feeling of being the bride—these are some of the things you can look forward to once the news that you're going to be married is out. But first, of course, you'll want to share your excitement with your family and friends. Imagine now the cry of joy from your roommate or the quiet smile that will tug at the corners of your father's mouth. Telling everyone is just the beginning of all the fun of a wedding.

Your Families First

Your families should be the first to hear the good news. How you go about letting them in on your decision is up to you.

If your parents know your fiancé extremely well, and he's

often visited their home, you might choose a time when you're all together, saying perhaps, "Dad, Mom . . . Bill and I have something we'd like to share with you. . . ." Chances are, you won't even get to finish your sentence—you'll be buried in good wishes! Living far away from your parents means you may not be able to wait to see them in person. In this case, do put in a joint telephone call. At the same time, make arrangements to visit your parents as soon as possible.

If your parents aren't acquainted with your fiancé yet, a letter or note asking them to please "invite someone very special" for a weekend or holiday works nicely. You needn't say anything until your fiancé feels comfortable and at home—rest assured, your parents will have a hint of your plans. (Incidentally, even if you are already sharing an apartment or house, you shouldn't expect to share a room in your parents' home if this makes them uneasy.) If your fiancé's schedule doesn't permit a visit or you're not sure how they'll react to your decision, then you might tell them of your upcoming marriage yourself, before you bring him into the picture.

No matter what your situation, your speaking with your family alone gives them—and you—the opportunity to express yourselves freely, crying a bit and laughing, and may seem the best way to inform them of your plans.

Your fiancé may still want to speak privately with your father. Not so much to ask for your hand—although some fathers appreciate this old-fashioned courtesy—as to receive congratulations, some loving thoughts about you, and a warm welcome to the family.

If your father is no longer alive, your mother, stepfather, guardian, or whoever raised you may talk with your fiancé. If your parents are divorced, he can see one parent, then the other.

He'll want, of course, to tell his parents right away, too. Again, how he lets them know is up to him. Once he does, his parents traditionally "call on" your parents, so everyone can get acquainted. His mother might drop your mother a note, or phone to invite your parents for drinks, brunch, or dinner. Any way his parents usually entertain their friends is a good way for them to get to know your parents. If your parents are divorced, your fiancé's family might first extend their invitation to the person who raised you. If your families live in different towns, a note from your fiancé's mother to your mother saying how pleased she is that you'll be a member of the family is a thoughtful gesture. In this case, your fiancé's parents may also ask you to spend a few days. Accept right away. Not only will you meet your fiancé's family, but if you haven't already, you may have a chance to see where he grew up, getting to know and appreciate the man you're marrying much better.

Even if your parents and his are old friends, this is the perfect excuse for them to have dinner together and toast the occasion. You two—and your brothers and sisters—may or may not be included. Now is the time for a small gathering. The bigger party can come when your engagement is officially announced.

Your fiancé's parents haven't contacted your parents? Then your mother might make the first move, perhaps calling to invite them over for a drink. There's no need to worry about custom, as long as the families are getting off to a good start.

Length of Engagement

You can consider yourselves engaged as soon as you decide to marry and to inform your parents. But you might wait to announce your engagement to everyone else until you begin making plans for your wedding (usually six to ten months before the ceremony; in some areas, up to a year). This may be a good idea if your fiancé has to complete his military service, or if you both look forward to graduating from college. Questions from well-meaning friends like, "When are you going to have your first baby?" and "How will you support yourselves?" start the moment the word of your upcoming marriage gets around. You may prefer some time to yourselves to settle issues like these between you, and to get to know one another as fully as you should in a relaxed way.

Publishing the News

Once you've decided to make your plans known to everyone, your engagement may be announced in your hometown newspapers. You and your parents may tell your closest friends and relatives somewhat before the announcement appears (rather than send printed cards, you should phone, speak, or write to them personally). Or you may time an engagement party for this purpose to coincide with the announcement release date.

Since policies vary from paper to paper, it's best to check with the society editor in advance about the proper form, deadlines, photograph requirements, and such. Some newspapers, for example, accept information over the phone, while others require that you submit a special printed form at least ten days prior to publication. Some papers publish wedding pictures only, while others publish either wedding or engagement pictures, but not both. Some will accept photographs of the engaged couple together. If your newspaper does not supply forms, send the necessary information to the society editor. Type it, double spaced, on one side of an 8½-x-11-inch sheet of paper. In the upper right-hand corner be sure to include the name, address, and phone number of your parents or someone in the community who can be contacted to verify the information. Include the date on which you would like the announcement to appear. Instead of indicating a Sunday —a very popular day—you might put under the phone number: "For release Wednesday, May 26, 1982."

The simplest and customary form:

Mr. and Mrs. Dennis Brown of Dayton Avenue announce the engagement of their daughter, Ann Marie, to Mr. John Smith, the son of Mr. and Mrs. Thomas Smith of St. Louis. No date has been set for the wedding. (Or, The wedding will take place in December.)

Notice the city is mentioned only when it is not the same as where the paper is published.

If your parents are divorced, the announcement is made by the parent with whom you've lived, but both parents are mentioned. (A divorced mother's name is traditionally a combination of her maiden and married surnames: "Mrs. Hoyt Brown." But she might prefer the more contemporary pairing of her given name and married surname: "Mrs. Jean Brown.")

Mrs. Hoyt Brown announces the engagement of her daughter, Ann Marie, to Mr. John Smith, the son of Mr. and Mrs. Thomas Smith of St. Louis. Miss Brown is also the daughter of Mr. Dennis Brown of Tulsa.

If your parents are divorced but friendly, they might wish to announce the news together:

Mr. Dennis Brown of Tulsa and Mrs. Hoyt Brown of Dayton Avenue, Chicago, announce the engagement of their daughter, Ann Marie, to Mr. John Smith, the son of Mr. and Mrs. Thomas Smith of St. Louis.

If your mother has remarried, she uses her current married name: "Mrs. Raymond Jones."

Mr. and Mrs. Raymond Jones announce the engagement of Mrs. Jones's daughter, Ann Marie Brown, to Mr. John Smith, the son of Mr. and Mrs. Thomas Smith of St. Louis. Miss Brown is also the daughter of Mr. Dennis Brown of Tulsa.

If one of your parents has died, your announcement might read:

The engagement of Miss Ann Marie Brown, daughter of Mrs. Dennis Brown and the late Mr. Brown, to Mr. John Smith, the son of Mr. and Mrs. Thomas Smith of St. Louis, is announced by the bride's mother.

If both of your parents are dead, the announcement is usually made by an older brother or sister or any close relative—even a close friend.

Mr. Jason Hoyt of Pittsburgh announces the engagement of his niece, Miss Ann Marie Brown, to Mr. John Smith, the son of Mr. and Mrs. Thomas Smith of St. Louis. Miss Brown is the daughter of the late Mr. and Mrs. Dennis Brown of Dayton Avenue.

Should your fiancé be the one whose parents are dead or divorced, you can adapt the appropriate wording to suit his situation.

It has not generally been the custom, but if you're marrying for the second time, an announcement may appear in your local newspapers. Word it in the usual way. There is no need to mention a previous marriage, although your newspaper may want to include this information. If, however, you've only been divorced a short while or your first spouse has died quite recently, wait and announce your wedding only.

Death in either family or someone critically ill means you will probably want to put off announcing your engagement until the worry has passed.

Information about military service, club memberships, or college associations may also be included, but there is no need to mention such facts unless they are usually printed in your newspaper. In some areas, it is also permissible to add a line indicating where gifts are registered—the society editor can also help with this. Listing a specific street address may invite theft.

If you send a photograph with your announcement, it should be an 8 x 10-inch glossy portrait (5 x 7 inches is also acceptable). Be sure to attach a line of identification and to protect your photo with a piece of stiff cardboard. A few newspapers have begun to charge fees for printing announcements; before you send anything in, check with the society editor on this.

An Engagement Party

Anyone may give a party in your honor, but your parents are the ones most likely to be looking forward to this pleasure. If they do have a party, it should be the first one celebrating your engagement. It may be held shortly before, after, or perhaps on the very day your engagement announcement appears in the newspapers.

Any sort of party gathering is appropriate: a buffet, a cocktail party, even a backyard picnic. "In honor of Howard and Carol" might be written on the invitations, and you two might greet guests in an informal receiving line with your parents and your fiancé's. Traditionally, it's not necessary for guests to bring gifts —and they probably won't if mention of the engagement is left off the invitation. This way, your parents can surprise everyone with the news at the party. Your father might choose a natural break to propose a toast to you and your fiancé. As whenever a toast is proposed to you, you refrain from raising your glass or taking even a sip. But after that, it's the custom for your fiancé to respond by drinking to you and your parents. Another toast from you might be a loving gesture.

Your fiancé's parents may want to give a party to introduce you to their family and friends, too. This might be a luncheon, a cocktail party, or a nice dinner, but it should not be a shower since the hosts this time are members of your groom's immediate family.

Be sure to thank in writing anyone who entertains for you, even if it has been as simple an outing as a picnic with brothers, sisters, cousins your own age. A sincere note, perhaps with a gift of flowers as well, will show everyone your thoughtfulness and consideration.

By the way, somewhere in among the partying, your mother-in-law-to-be will probably suggest, "Oh, call me Marjorie!" (Or "Mom" or "Mother B.") Or she may ask you what you would like to call her. You might suggest her first name or whatever your fiancé calls her, unless that is what you call your own mother. She hasn't brought it up? If you're still feeling a bit unsure in your relationship with her, have your fiancé drop a gentle suggestion. But chances are, you'll be comfortable enough to say, "We're getting to know one another really well, and you've already made me feel like a part of your family. Jack calls you Mom —may I call you Mom, too?"

Engagement Presents

Your first engagement gift will probably be your ring, though a ring is not necessary to being engaged. A single diamond symbolizing love and fidelity is the classic choice, but other precious and semiprecious stones—from opals to emeralds—are also beautifully appropriate. When your budget is very limited, you may prefer to do without the engagement ring in favor of a really handsome wedding ring; some couples (men and women alike) choose engagement rings they will wear as wedding rings, too. Your engagement ring needn't be new. Your fiancé may wish to honor you with an heirloom ring from his family, or to have family stones reset in a style you select.

You do not have to give your fiancé an engagement gift, but many brides choose to do so. It is usually something personal and

lasting, perhaps a wristwatch or leather-bound edition of his favorite book. In addition to your ring—or in place of it—your
fiancé may give you another gift. Such a gift may be anything
you like, though items that indicate financial or material support
(money, cars, clothing) aren't in the strictest tradition.

As far as family and friends are concerned, an engagement
need not be a gift-giving occasion. But those particularly close to
you may surprise you with household or trousseau items. Whatever you receive, respond promptly with a written note of thanks,
even if you expressed your appreciation in person when you
opened the gift.

Broken Engagements

If you decide to call off your engagement, send a release to
every newspaper that published your announcement, stating
quite simply:

*The engagement of Miss Ann Marie Brown and Mr.
John Smith has been terminated by mutual consent.*

Return any gifts that were given you for your engagement,
including your ring. Your former fiancé's family will especially
appreciate getting back any heirlooms that may have been given
to you, but you may keep any other birthday or holiday presents
you have received.

If it's a last-minute decision, wedding invitations will have to
be recalled by notes, telephone calls, or telegrams (see Chapter 5),
and all wedding gifts returned. A brief personal note from you to
close family friends and relatives is thoughtful, but there is no
need to go into details.

In the unfortunate case of a fiancé's death before the wedding,

the gifts must also be returned. Someone in the bride's family
may assume this task, in consideration of the bride's feelings and
those of the fiancé's parents and other relatives.

Weddings and Parents

A wedding is a tradition as much for parents, in a sense, as it
is for the couple. Not only will a man and woman look at themselves and one another in a different way once they are husband
and wife, but their parents will as well. Marriage means two people are taking new roles in society. Marking this occasion with a
special celebration makes it easier for everyone to adjust. Couples
who choose not to involve parents, and parents who wish, whatever the reason, not to involve themselves fail to help the adjustment process along. Even if there are misgivings, after they have
been voiced, they should be put aside. And everyone should try
to take part in the plans. No matter how small and intimate the
ceremony, a wedding is a time of transition, a time for building
toward happy relationships in the future.

2
Wedding Customs

Wedding customs evolve from a wish to symbolize all the good things marriage means to the couple and to their community: happiness, commitment, sharing. Every culture has its own wedding customs. The old ones are updated to accommodate changing values and ideals, new ones are created to enrich everyone's experience of the marriage celebration.

Your wedding dress, your veil, your flowers, all have traditional significance and, in a way, mean as much to others as they mean to you. Here are the whys and wherefores of many of our modern American marriage tradition.

Contemporary Customs, Their Whys and Wherefores

Why an engagement ring? The betrothal ring dates back to the days of marriage by purchase, when it served as both partial payment for the bride and as a symbol of the groom's honorable intentions. The diamond, first incorporated into engagement rings in medieval Italy, was, because of its hardness, chosen to stand for enduring love. Now that men and women are enjoying equal roles in their relationships, a bride may be as likely to give an engagement ring to her groom as vice versa.

Why a wedding ring? The circular shape of the wedding ring has suggested unending love since the days of the early Egyptians. Primitive brides wore rings of rushes or hemp which had to be replaced every year. Early Romans chose more durable iron to symbolize the permanence of marriage. The current favorite is, of course, gold, with its lasting beauty and purity. And, again, husbands as well as wives now wear wedding bands proudly—and forever.

Why the third finger, left hand? Ancient peoples believed that the vein in the third finger of the left hand ran directly to the heart. Medieval bridgerooms placed the ring on three of the bride's fingers in turn to symbolize the trinity: "the Father, the Son, and the Holy Spirit." The ring remained on the third finger, and that has since become the customary ring finger for all English-speaking cultures. However, in many European countries, the wedding ring is worn on the right hand. A Greek woman wears her ring on her left hand until she is married, moving it to her right hand after.

Why the bridal shower? Tradition has it that the first bridal shower took place in Holland when a maiden fell in love with a poor miller. Her father forbade the marriage, denying her the customary bridal dowry. So the miller's friends "showered" the bride with gifts to help the young couple set up housekeeping.

Why does the bride wear a veil? Originally, the bride's veil symbolized her youth and virginity. Even today, in some countries, the groom meets his bride veiled and never sees her face until after the wedding. Early Greek and Roman brides wore flame red veils. Early Christian brides wore white or purple. It is said that Nelly Custis began the fashion for the lacy, white veil of today when she chose to wear a long scarf to her wedding to President Washington's aide, Major Lawrence Lewis. Her decision stemmed from the flattering comments her fiancé made after glimpsing her through a lace curtain at an open window. Fresh or silk flowers caught with a wisp of veil, or a hat tied with veiling, is a modern interpretation of this wedding classic.

Why does the bride wear white? White has been a symbol of celebration since Roman times. At the turn of the twentieth century, it stood for purity as well. Today, since women marrying again may choose among the many shades of white, it holds its original meaning of happiness and joy.

Why does the bride carry flowers? Flowers have long stood for a variety of emotions and values—lilies for virtue, roses for love, and so on. Early Roman brides carried bunches of herbs under their veils to symbolize fidelity. The Greeks used ivy as a sign of indissoluble love. Our modern orange blossoms were chosen by the Saracens to represent fulfillment and happiness, as the orange tree blooms and bears fruit at the same time.

Why something blue? The brides of ancient Israel wore a blue ribbon on the border of their fringed robes to denote modesty, fidelity, and love—ideals still associated with that color. Blue is also the color that represents the purity of the Virgin Mary. Besides its symbolic value, blue is probably the most popular of all colors.

Why the trousseau? Derived from the French word *trousse*, meaning bundle, the trousseau originated as a bundle of clothing and personal possessions the bride carried with her to her new home. This was later expanded into a more generous dowry that enhanced the value of an unmarried daughter in the eyes of prospective suitors. Today, the trousseau encompasses all of the new things—for the household and for the couple themselves—that help make the transition to a new stage of life.

Why is the bride given away? She isn't always. In fact, many people nowadays confuse the part of the marriage ceremony where the bride is escorted to the altar with the "giving away"—where the person officiating asks, "Who gives this woman to be married?" In earlier times, when women were granted fewer personal rights, the bride was literally given to the groom in an arranged marriage. But the bride of today who keeps the "giving away" in her marriage service often sees it as symbolic of her parents' support for her union and their promise of continued trust and affection. Many a couple have adapted this custom by having both sets of parents bless the marriage, along with the clergy.

Why a wedding cake? Cake has been a part of wedding celebrations since Roman times when a thin loaf was broken over the bride's head at the close of the ceremony. The wheat from which it was made symbolized fertility; the crumbs were eagerly sought by guests as good luck charms. During the Middle Ages, it was traditional for the bride and groom to kiss over a pile of small cakes. When an enterprising baker decided to mass all these cakes together and cover them with frosting, the modern, tiered wedding cake was born.

Why rice and old shoes? In the Orient, rice means, "May you always have a full pantry," and a red slipper thrown onto the roof of a house indicates that a honeymoon is in progress. Also, among early Hebrews, sandals were often exchanged as evidence of good faith in the sale of property. Today, casting a shoe after the bride signifies carrying on the devotion she has for her parents to include her husband, while the rice remains as a token of a life of plenty.

Why a honeymoon? In ancient marriages by capture, the groom kept his bride in hiding to prevent searching relatives from finding her. The term *honeymoon* had its origin when early Teuton couples drank a honey drink, known as mead or metheglin, for thirty days after their wedding or until the moon had waned.

Why is the bride carried over the threshold? The Roman bride, demonstrating her reluctance to leave her father's home, had to be dragged over the threshold to her new house. It was also believed that evil spirits hovered at the threshold of the new house, so the bride was lifted over to ensure her protection from them.

Traditions Around the World

Along with these customs that have been woven into our American wedding heritage, you may want to personalize your celebration with customs from other countries, perhaps those of your and your fiancé's ancestors. Here are some ideas.

Africa: Some tribes still perform the ancient rite of binding bride's and groom's wrists together with plaited grass. Show your new ties by holding hands as you take that walk back up the aisle together as husband and wife.

Belgium: The bride of long ago would stitch her name on her bridal-day handkerchief, frame it, and keep it till it was time for the next family bride to marry. Share this tradition with your attendants—embroider a handkerchief for each one of them to treasure and hand down to their families.

Bermuda: Even today islanders top off their tiered wedding cakes with a tiny tree sapling. The newlyweds plant the tree at the reception. Put your little tree in a place where you both can watch it grow along with your marriage.

China: The color of love and joy in Old China—red—was once the favorite choice for the bride's dress, candles, gift boxes, and her money envelopes. Tuck a red rosebud in your groom's lapel, wrap maids' gifts in red paper—for color and for luck.

Czechoslovakia: Brides in the countryside carry on a very old custom—wearing wreaths of rosemary woven for them on their wedding eve. Include a sprig in your bouquet for wisdom, love, and loyalty.

England: The village bride and her wedding party always used to walk together to the church. Leading the procession: a small girl strewing blossoms along the road so the bride's path through life would always be happy and flower-laden. Walk to your reception site if it's nearby; and if you've young friends or are parents marrying again, let the children head the parade.

Finland: Brides once wore golden crowns. After the wedding, unmarried women danced around the blindfolded bride. Whoever she crowned would marry next. Change your headpiece to a garland of flowers at your reception. If you choose the next bride-to-be the same way, you can save your bouquet as a memento.

France: As did newlyweds of days past, many couples drink the reception toast from an engraved two-handled cup (the *coupe de mariage*) which will be passed on to future generations. You might begin shopping now for the perfect silver cup to engrave with your initials so that you'll be sure to have it in time for a champagne toast at your reception.

Germany: Both bride and groom hold candles trimmed with flowers and ribbons. Planning a late afternoon or evening wedding? Then say your vows by candle-glow, too—save one of the tapers to relight for a romantic first-anniversary dinner.

Hawaii: Marry at a sacred place still popular with Hawaiian Americans like one of many natural caves feathered by giant ferns. Do the next best thing if you can't marry in Hawaii. Honeymoon there!

Holland: Dutch families used to plan a party prior to the wedding. Bride and groom would sit on thrones under a canopy of fragrant evergreens—for everlasting love. One by one the guests came up to offer their good wishes. Why don't you host an informal buffet or barbecue for all your out-of-town guests, or ask a friend to give a breakfast on the wedding morning. Introduce them all around so they'll get to know everyone before the wedding.

India: The groom's brother sprinkles flower petals on the bridal couple at the end of the ceremony. After your ceremony is over—or before—have a special family member or friend hand a single flower to every guest.

Iran: When this country was called Persia, the groom bought the wedding dress—ten yards of sheeting to wrap 'round and 'round his bride. Not your style? Then ask your groom to remember the old tradition with a token gift . . . a white wedding handkerchief to complete your wedding ensemble.

Ireland: The traditional wedding cake of the Emerald Isle is not a delicate white cake but a heavy and rich fruitcake with golden raisins, ground almonds, cherries, and spice. In true Irish spirit, lace the recipe with brandy or bourbon.

Italy: Wedding guests have for centuries tossed *confetti*, sugared almonds, at the new couple. Decorate your reception tables with pretty little boxes or bags brimming with almonds—favors your guests will love.

Japan: Bridal couples will take nine sips of *sake*, becoming husband and wife after the first sip. Borrow a Japanese reception tradition for your ceremony. After you and your groom drink from the wine cup, ask your parents and his to exchange sips to show the close new ties between your two families.

Mexico: Guests at many Mexican weddings love observing a reception tradition—they gather around the couple in a heart-shaped ring. Your guests might do the same as you whirl through your first dance together as husband and wife.

Norway: After a reindeer-kabob dinner lit by the midnight sun, certain nomadic tribes have always done what everyone at your wedding will do if you plan a big reception with a band— dance the night away.

Poland: Many reception guests have customarily pinned money on the bride and groom to buy a dance. Collect your pin money in a white satin purse. (You can make it or find one where you'll buy your dress.)

Rumania: Practicing a custom similar to those in several countries, guests toss sweets and nuts at the new couple to wish them prosperity. Make up packets of birdseed for your guests to throw, a wedding feast for wrens and robins.

Russia: Wedding guests don't only give presents—they get them! Favor your guests with tiny picture frames, bud vases, instant photos of themselves.

Spain: In certain regions long ago, the bride wore a black silk dress and mantilla, orange blossoms for the hair. For the groom: a tucked shirt hand-embroidered by the bride. Try a lacy white mantilla for your headpiece and gift your groom with a shirt to go with his formal wear, after hand-embroidering his initials on the cuff.

Sweden: To frighten away trolls (imaginary beasts who were once thought to bring misfortune), bridesmaids carried bouquets of pungent herbs—and the groom sewed thyme into his clothes. You might include fragrant lavender in your bouquet.

Switzerland: The junior bridesmaid leads the procession to the reception with handfuls of colored handkerchiefs for the guests. Whoever wants a handkerchief contributes a coin toward your first nest egg.

Wales: The bride gives her attendants cuttings of myrtle from her bouquet. Tell your maids that if their plants bloom—another wedding!

More "old-country" traditions can be discovered by talking with your librarian, older relatives, or religious officials. Jewish couples the world over, for instance, pledge a life together under a *huppah*, a canopy of embroidered cloth or flowers, to symbolize the home they will share. The groom smashes a wine glass under his heel as a reminder that in marriage there are times of sorrow amidst the joy, and the couple may sign an elaborately embellished *ketubah*, or marriage contract with the husband's promises to his wife, which is hung in a prominent place in the home.

And no matter what your heritage or faith, you'll certainly want to follow the ancient British wedding rhyme and wear "something old, something new, something borrowed, something blue, and a lucky penny in your shoe."

3
Pre-Wedding Parties

You'll probably attend more parties during your engagement than at any other time in your life. Some, like the traditional maids' luncheon, you'll host yourself. But most, other people will give for you. You and your fiancé may be honored at anything from a picnic on stadium blankets to an elegant dinner with orchids and damask, over quiet cups of tea or high-spirited cocktails, at dawn near the beach or at midnight after the theater. Your only responsibilities are to show everyone how very much you are enjoying yourself, and to follow up each event with a note of thanks, and flowers, perhaps, to your hostess or host. You might also tactfully see to it that no guest is invited to so many parties that he or she ends up feeling pinched for time or money. And guard your own energy—especially the last week or two before the wedding—so you will be rested and relaxed on this most important day.

Showers

Showers are parties with a purpose, given to help the couple outfit their new home or assemble a trousseau. They have traditionally been given by women who are good friends of the bride, sometimes by a relative, most often by the honor attendant or bridesmaids. Today, of course, a married couple, even the best man, might host these parties. In fact, anyone who knows you may give a shower, except members of your or your groom's immediate families (your mother or sister, or his brother, for example); they're so close to you both it would seem as if you were asking for presents.

The party itself may be almost any type, at any time that's convenient for you and your host or hostess, although you may prefer that the last week before the wedding be kept free. With so many women working, the shower is as likely to be held in a restaurant at night as someone's house during the day. Whenever or wherever, showers are almost always informal, with a light menu and the emphasis on your pleasure as you open and exclaim over your presents.

The host or hostess issues invitations by telephone, mail, or in person. People who do not know you may be left off the guest list, even though they may be friends of your family or your fiancé's. The usual guest list includes your honor attendant and bridesmaids, along with your and your groom's mothers, sisters, and other close relatives. (Showers given by co-workers, club members, or school friends mean only members of that group will probably be on hand.) Today, showers may be for couples, with the groom and his close friends, the husbands and special dates of other guests also invited—this is becoming more and more popular both because men are taking a greater interest in the home, and because it's so much fun!

When several showers are planned, the guest list should be different for each one so no one ends up having to buy several shower gifts, a wedding gift, and possibly a bridesmaid's outfit as well. In a small community, or when you know that many people are eager to honor you, it is considerate to suggest that people join together to host just one general shower instead of several small ones. Should yet another friend flatter you with the news she's planning a shower, though, remember she's already put a lot of thought into it. Thank her, and say something like, "You know Dorothy Murray and Sally Lowe? They're having a shower too— I'd love to give you their numbers. It would be terrific for me if there could be one shower where I'll get to see all of you together before the wedding." The thoughtful bride who has planned a formal wedding also sees to it, if possible, that people not invited to the wedding are not put in the position of being asked to a shower.

Every shower guest brings a gift. And since gift-giving will always be an expression of individuality, the gifts will be as unique as your hometown and your heritage. That is as it should be. But traditionally, shower gifts have been small and relatively inexpensive—like mixing bowls and bar tools. (If you list your preferences at your store's wedding gift registry, it would be a courtesy to potential shower guests to include small items such as wooden spoons in addition to more expensive items such as a blender and toaster.) Another alternative is the joint or group gift, like a vacuum cleaner or lacy nightgown and peignoir set, toward which all the guests contribute. The hostess collects the money and makes the purchase, seeing to it that in cases where incomes vary widely, no guest contributes more than he or she can afford. If you would prefer one major gift to many small ones, you might drop a discreet hint to the right person (your mother or honor attendant, perhaps).

Shower Themes

Kitchen showers, bath showers, plant, book, or travel showers. The possibilities are endless. If you've something special in mind, let that "right person" know. Otherwise, trust to the good judgment of your hostess.

Kitchen showers are probably the most popular theme because

of the enormous range of paraphernalia every couple can use. Novice cooks—especially those who've never kept house on their own—need everything from pots and pans, small appliances and utensils, to wastebaskets, mops, brooms, and sponges. One variation on the kitchen theme has each guest bringing a favorite recipe along with one item needed for its preparation (a flour sifter with a cake recipe). If the hostess sends out uniform recipe cards in advance, she can assemble them all into one easy-to-use recipe box or notebook.

All-female showers are naturals for frilly night things and underwear, sewing accessories, closet or drawer organizers, and certificates for the ultimate in beauty treatments and products.

Showers for couples lend themselves to magazine subscriptions, green plants, liquor and mixes, books and records, sporting gear, and games.

It is the hostess's job to plan a party that complements both theme and guests: a pool party or backyard barbecue for a coed group; a champagne brunch or pastel-pretty luncheon for all women; a cocktail party or buffet or hors d'oeuvres for a gathering that's both young and old.

Naturally your exuberant "thank-yous" contribute to the fun of the party, but you should follow up with notes to each guest. At one time, notes weren't considered necessary when you thanked someone in person. But now, with showers growing bigger and people getting busier, a personal note is the only way to make sure your sincere words of appreciation won't get lost in the crowd. If your groom attended the party, of course, he might write his own notes to those special friends of his you don't know as well.

Bridesmaids' Parties

It is customary for the bridesmaids—individually or together—to entertain for the bride. But this isn't required. And if they contribute to a shower, you are sure to enjoy it as much as any other party. You may treat your maids to a party, of course—the traditional luncheon, an afternoon tea, or even a chili-and-beer supper held at your home or neighborhood pub. Again, it doesn't matter so much what kind of celebration it is; the important thing is that everyone feels comfortable enough to have a good time. Whoever is hosting, the maids party is the perfect time to introduce out-of-town attendants, schedule final dress fittings, display your wedding gifts, and distribute your presents to your maids. They may also present their gifts to you.

There's a delightful tradition you might want to observe that goes along with any maids' party: Serve a pink cake for dessert with a ring, coin, or thimble baked inside. Legend says the maid whose slice of cake contains the trinket will be the next to wed. Just imagine the teasing and laughing if your little sister—the one who swears she'll never get married—ends up with the prize!

The Bachelor Party

The bachelor dinner is another optional custom. But it has quite a reputation as a chance for the groom and his attendants to release their pre-wedding tensions. The bachelor dinner may be hosted by either the groom's friends or by the groom himself. It is the perfect time for him, too, to pass out his gifts to his ushers and best man and to settle any last-minute details.

At some point during the party, usually just after dinner, the groom proposes a champagne toast to his bride. Traditionally each man then smashes his glass so it may never be used for a less worthy purpose—if the party is held at a restaurant or club, arrangements for following this custom should be made ahead of time. As more drinking inevitably follows, it is wise to suggest that the bachelor party be scheduled a few days before the actual ceremony so everyone has time to recover.

To any bride: Don't nag about what happened at the bachelor

party (probably nothing much did). A little good-natured needling might not hurt, however. Your fiancé may have practiced a great comeback, and you wouldn't want to disappoint him.

The Rehearsal Dinner

The wedding rehearsal is generally followed up with a dinner for members of the wedding party. In many locales, the groom's parents, or any other close relatives or friends, may also do the honors. All your attendants (except very young children), your and your fiancé's immediate families, and the ceremony official (with spouse, if any) usually attend, along with any out-of-town guests, family, and friends you, or the host, wishes to invite.

This dinner may be held at a private home or in a restaurant, club, or hotel, and it may be as informal as the host would like, or as elegant, as long as the wedding remains the main attraction. At some point, the best man usually offers a toast to the bride and groom. The groom may follow with a toast to you and your parents. You might, if you want, lift your glass to him and his parents next, with a toast like, "To my future husband, and to his mother and father. They raised a man so special, I couldn't help but say yes." The dining and drinking can go on for hours. If you've not already done so, pass out your attendants' gifts. After thanking everyone, just the two of you might then slip away early to rest for the big day.

The Wedding Breakfast

Hosted by a friend or neighbor in honor of all those who've come from out of town for the occasion, the wedding-day breakfast or brunch is a wonderful way to occupy and entertain guests who may feel in need of a warm welcome. Neither you nor your groom and your families are expected to attend, so you can take care of last-minute wedding-day preparations. Therefore, you might suggest hosting the breakfast to a relative or friend in town who has offered to help out with some aspect of the planning along the way.

The more people you talk to about your upcoming wedding, the more you will realize that it is just the excuse they have been waiting for to have a really good time themselves.

4
Planning Your Wedding

A beautiful formal wedding—the kind most couples and their families dream of—takes six to ten months to plan, up to a year in big cities and their suburbs. For even the simplest and most intimate ceremony and reception, you'll need two to three months. So one of the first things you'll need to decide is when, where, and how you'll marry.

When and Where

To set the precise date and time of your ceremony, you'll have to consider certain religious observances and local customs, as well as the degree of formality you wish and the number of weddings being planned for the same time period. Some faiths, for example, do not allow formal weddings on certain days of the calendar. Others perform wedding ceremonies only during certain hours. Caterers, too, are frequently overbooked, so you must make sure your reception site will be available on the date you choose. June is the classic month for weddings, and very popular, as are August, September, and the winter holiday season. Incidentally, the earlier you begin your planning, the more time you will have to compare services and choose those best-suited to your wedding budget.

You may choose almost any location for your wedding—a small, college chapel; a vast cathedral with spires and stained glass; stately and dignified judge's chambers; a glamorous hotel ballroom; the home where you grew up; your grandmother's garden; even a public park or the grounds of some of the prettier new apartment or condominium developments. Your religious beliefs and the number of guests you expect are the main considerations in selecting a site. A civil ceremony at city hall meets all the legal requirements, but you'll be limited in the number of guests you can invite. A home or chapel is quite suitable for a small wedding, but a Catholic church may be an easier place to celebrate a Nuptial Mass. A Jewish wedding will be lovely in a synagogue or temple, but in some areas, large ceremonies are held at clubs or hotels.

You and your fiancé need not be active members of a congregation in order to have a religious wedding. Some churches will rent all or part of their facilities for a fee. Do check with a representative of the church in advance, however, as some religions will not honor the marriage of people who are of different faiths or who have divorced or who prefer not to attend special premarital discussions with the clergy. (In these cases, friends, a campus ministry group, or an ethical society may guide you to an appropriate house of worship.)

As the bride, you have the prerogative of choosing the wedding site, and it is customary for the ceremony to take place in your hometown. But naturally you'll want to regard the wishes of your groom, your parents, and his. If you and your fiancé live in a city far from both sets of parents, for example, it may make more sense to be married there among your mutual friends. A reception immediately following, and another party later near the home of your parents will assure that no one's friends and relatives feel left out.

What Type of Wedding

There are four basic types of weddings: very formal, formal, semiformal, and informal. Knowing which style you and your families prefer will help you plan an overall atmosphere where everyone feels comfortable and has a wonderful time. The current or past lifestyles of the couple needn't influence greatly the kind of wedding decided upon—the bride in a long white dress or the engraved announcement of marriage, for example, are parts of the wedding celebration so long loved. Garden weddings, military weddings, double weddings, and of course, weddings that are personalized in any way may be variations of the basic types.

A VERY FORMAL WEDDING usually includes:

A stately dress with a cathedral- or chapel-length train and veil for the bride.

Formal attire (traditional white tie and tails in the evening, cutaways in the daytime, or contemporary black, contoured long or short jackets, and wing-collared shirts) for the groom and men in the wedding party.

Four to twelve bridesmaids in floor-length dresses.

Long dresses for the mothers of the bride and groom.

A high noon, late afternoon, or evening ceremony.

200 or more guests.

Engraved or printed invitations, generally with the traditional wording, and separate reception invitations enclosed.

A large and lavish reception, usually with a seated meal.

A FORMAL WEDDING usually calls for:

A long dress with a chapel or sweep train; a veil or veiled hat for the bride.

Formal clothes (traditional black tie in the evening, stroller jackets with striped trousers in the daytime, or contemporary colored formal suits) for the groom and his attendants.

Two to six bridesmaids, usually in long dresses.

Long or elaborate street-length dresses for the mothers.

Ceremony at any hour of the day, perhaps personalized with a couple's own vows, songs, and such.

At least 100 guests.

Engraved or printed invitations, with either traditional or personalized wordings (response cards may or may not be included).

A most festive reception—food and beverages appropriate to the hour.

A SEMIFORMAL WEDDING usually means:

An elaborate street-length or simple floor-length dress in white or pastel with a hat, hair flowers, or short veil for the bride.

Dark suits with four-in-hand ties, dinner jackets, or contemporary formal suits for the groom and his attendants, depending on the hour.

One or two bridal attendants in street-length or cocktail-length dresses.

Street-length or cocktail-length dresses for the mothers.

A morning, early afternoon, or later evening ceremony.

Fewer than 100 guests.

A single engraved or printed invitation to both the ceremony and reception.

An intimate reception, with light refreshment.

AN INFORMAL WEDDING is usually characterized by:

Street clothes, often a lovely suit or jacketed dress for the bride.

Suits for the groom and best man.

A maid or matron of honor, but no bridesmaids, in street clothes.

A daytime ceremony anywhere, including city hall.

A guest list including relatives and close friends.

50 or fewer guests.

Handwritten or personal invitations to both the ceremony and the reception.

In general, the formality of a wedding increases with the size of the guest list. But a wedding before fifty guests in a magnificent church might still have you enjoying the regal feeling of formal dress. Or several hundred guests might join you for a joyous, informal celebration in a meadow or on a hilltop.

What Type of Reception

Large or small, formal or not, it is best if your reception immediately follows the ceremony and is of a style that complements your wedding theme. For example, you might serve a light luncheon or brunch after a morning wedding, cake and punch or cocktails and hors d'oeuvres following an afternoon ceremony. Late afternoon and evening weddings are often accompanied by dinner with dancing or a large cocktail-buffet party. A wedding cake and champagne or punch for toasting are the only reception requirements. Since it is most courteous to offer guests the kind of reception fare their appetites will expect at the hour of the day, this guideline can give a clue to trimming costs. Serving only cake and punch to 300 guests will seem more natural at 3:00 P.M. than at 6:00 P.M.

You may hold your reception almost anywhere, from the church fellowship hall to your own home or backyard to a private club, hotel, or restaurant. Adequate kitchen facilities, sufficient space for the comfort of all your guests, and accessible parking and transportation are the only limitations.

Ideally, of course, you'll invite all your guests to both the ceremony and the reception. But it is quite proper to follow an intimate family ceremony with a large reception for your friends. After all, a reception is a party—a time to have fun!

Visiting Your Clergy or Judge

As soon as you've decided when and where you wish to marry, make an appointment to visit the person you would like to officiate—minister, priest, rabbi, or judge. This is not only the practical thing to do, it is the requirement in many religions.

Unless you are both members of the same church, you may have to show certificates of baptism or confirmation, and perhaps a letter attesting to your marital or religious status. If you are of different faiths, you may need to get a special dispensation and arrange to have religious instruction before your wedding.

In any case, you will have to confirm your ceremony date. Have several choices in mind, since it is often necessary to reserve your day and time several months in advance, and popular churches and halls may already be booked on your chosen date.

You'll also want to go over the details of the wedding ceremony and clarify clergy preferences on music, photography, and decoration. If you would like any changes in the standard text, or wish to write your own ceremony, this is the time to discuss your plans. Couples hoping to personalize the wedding service are often surprised that the clergy are an enormous source of ideas—do take advantage of their help.

Sometimes, however, a concerned official will bring up a topic you feel is too personal to discuss. If you and your fiancé find yourselves in this situation, a polite response might be, "You brought up some good questions. Mark and I have been talking about this a lot. But this is something we prefer to do in private." Then steer the conversation back to a subject that is more comfortable for everyone.

It is a good idea to arrange to speak with the sexton, verger, or church secretary as well. He or she can explain the fire laws governing evening candlelight ceremonies, for example, and tell you all about aisle carpets, prayer benches, canopies, and any other special equipment you might need. You can make arrangements for your rehearsal or for reserved parking spaces, too.

You'll also want to see the church organist to discuss your musical program, get advice and suggestions, and make sure the organist will be available for both your ceremony and rehearsal. If additional musicians or a soloist will perform, it may be smart to schedule extra rehearsals to make sure the timing is perfect. (For some musical selections, see Chapter 13.)

Your Marriage License

All states require a marriage license, and you can apply together for your license at your local county clerk's office two to three weeks before your wedding. But, first, call ahead to find out what your state's specifications are. Usually you will need proof that you are of age or have parental consent to marry, proof of citizenship if you were not born in the United States, and doctor's certificates verifying the results of any necessary blood tests or physical examinations. There is often a waiting period (two to three days) before the license is valid, and it is good for a maximum time limit (about thirty days). Keep this limit in mind when you make a date to get the license. Working couples might take a half-day off, and afterward, celebrate with a lingering lunch at their favorite restaurant.

Selecting Your Rings

Shopping together for the engagement and wedding rings assures that both you and your groom will be pleased with the choices. Wedding bands may be chosen to match the engagement ring or to be worn alone. The bride's rings may or may not match the groom's, but all rings should be bought with an eye to flattering the hands that will wear them. If you wish your rings engraved, you may decide on either the traditional inscription of the bride's maiden-name initials, the groom's initials, and the wedding date, in that order ("R.G.S. from J.R.B. 6/12/80"), or any other sentimental phrase that fits in the space available. If you plan a double-ring ceremony, your honor attendant will hold the groom's ring, the best man will hold yours, until they are exchanged during the ceremony.

Who Pays for What

The bride's family is traditionally responsible for the wedding ceremony, and the cost of the reception as well. Nowadays, however, the couple themselves may contribute to the overall budget. The groom's family may also offer to share in the costs—and the bride's family may politely decline or accept as they wish. In this case, having the bill for one or two specific items—such as all the flowers or all the reception beverages—sent directly to the groom's family (rather than having them take care of a percentage of total costs) is the most pleasant arrangement. It is probably best if the groom's parents who volunteer to handle some expenses not ask for special accommodations—more guests or an open bar, for instance. If the groom's parents would like to host a party for the couple after the wedding, this will give them the opportunity to entertain in the style familiar to them, their relatives, and friends. Traditionally, again, the costs are divided as outlined below.

THE BRIDE (OR HER FAMILY) PAYS FOR:

Invitations, announcements, and enclosures.

Wedding dress, veil, and accessories.

Trousseau of clothes and lingerie.

Bouquets or corsages for honor attendant, bridesmaids, and flower girl.

Flowers for the ceremony and reception sites.

Engagement and wedding photographs.

Rental fee (if any) for the church.

Fees for the sexton, organist, and soloist.

Rental of aisle carpet, marquee, and other equipment.

Transportation of the bridal party to the ceremony and reception sites.

Complete reception, including all food, beverages, music, decorations, gratuities, and professional services.

Groom's ring (or rings).

Wedding gift for the groom.

Gifts for bride's attendants.

Hotel lodging (if necessary) for any bridesmaids from out-of-town.

Bride's personal writing paper.

THE GROOM (OR HIS FAMILY) PAYS FOR:

Bride's engagement and wedding rings.

Marriage license.

Ceremony official's fee (usually ranging from $10 to $100 for the clergy; for a judge, a suitable gift may be all that's necessary).

Bride's flowers, including going-away corsage and bouquet (see below).

Wedding gift for the bride.

Gifts for the best man and ushers.

Hotel lodging (if necessary) for out-of-town ushers.

Complete wedding trip.

EXPENSES WHICH ARE OPTIONAL OR SET BY LOCAL CUSTOM:

Bride's bouquet—traditionally a gift from the groom, but may be included in the bridal outfit supplied by her family.

Flowers for mothers and grandmothers—usually provided by the groom, but the bride may buy those for her own mother and grandmothers.

Attendants' dresses—usually bought by each maid, but the bride may provide them if she chooses.

Bridemaids' party—usually given by the bride, but may be given by her attendants or relatives.

Bachelors' party—given by the groom's attendants and friends in most places, but may also be given by the groom.

Rehearsal dinner—given by the groom's family in most communities, but may also be hosted by relatives or friends of the bride.

Bride's Reminder List

A formal wedding takes several months to plan. You may postpone or eliminate some of the usual preparations if you have a smaller wedding, but for a traditional large celebration, it is best to get everything done as soon as possible. The following reminder list is based on a six-month schedule. However, if you live in a metropolitan area, you may need to allow ten months to a year, and adjust the schedule accordingly.

SIX MONTHS before your wedding:

Buy (or begin) a wedding planning book or memory album.

Discuss wedding budget with your parents; if you'll share expenses, include your fiancé and his parents. Even if you won't divide costs, talk about the wedding style with everyone—everything from flowers to food to beverages to dancing.

Decide where your wedding and reception will take place.

Determine the number of guests you can accommodate and start making out your guest list. Have your fiancé and his family start making out theirs. Remember that guests invited to the ceremony should also be invited to the reception.

Plan the color scheme for your ceremony and reception.

Visit your minister or other officiating authority with your fiancé.

Plan your reception and make the necessary reservations with the caterer, musicians, etc. (See Chapter 12.)

Choose your wedding dress, veil, and accessories, arranging a delivery date so you will have your complete outfit in time for your bridal portrait (about one month before the wedding).

Shop with your fiancé for your engagement ring.

Select your dinnerware, flatware, glassware, and other household items and register your choices with your favorite store.

Discuss with your fiancé how many attendants you will have and begin to choose them.

Start planning your new home and begin your household shopping.

Set the date to order the attendants' dresses and headpieces.

Discuss honeymoon plans with your fiancé so reservations can be made. If you plan to travel outside the country, check on passports, visas, and inoculations.

THREE MONTHS before your wedding:

Complete your guest list and check it for duplication with your fiancé's.

Read Chapter 5 carefully, then order invitations and any announcements and enclosure cards, allowing at least four weeks for printing.

Pick up invitation envelopes in advance and begin addressing them so they'll be ready for mailing as soon as the invitations are delivered.

Order your personal writing paper. (See the section on thank-you notes in Chapter 16.)

Discuss your wedding color scheme with your mother so she can choose her dress. (She can then advise the groom's mother on length, color, and style for her dress.)

Confirm delivery date of your dress, and if you haven't already, make the final selection of the attendants' dresses.

Make appointments for fittings.

Begin shopping for your personal trousseau.

Engage a photographer for wedding-day candids.

Arrange for your bridal portrait with a photographer other than the candid photographer, if you like.

Make an appointment for a physical examination and any tests you'll need for your marriage license.

Discuss ceremony details with organist, sexton, etc.

Firm up reception plans with the person in charge.

Consult with your florist and order flowers that are suitable to the wedding color scheme and season as well.

ONE MONTH before your wedding:

Mail your invitations, recording acceptances and regrets as they arrive. Send out maps, if not included in the invitations, but requested, and pew cards, if needed, to those who accept. Begin addressing your announcements.

Have the final fitting of your dress and headpiece.

Have your wedding portrait taken.

Choose and order the gifts for your attendants.

Select the groom's wedding ring, wedding present, too, if you are exchanging them.

Order your wedding cake if it's not included in the catering service.

Arrange accommodations for relatives and attendants from out of town.

Plan the bridesmaids' party if you'll be giving it.

Discuss arrangements for the rehearsal dinner with the hosts.

Write thank-you notes for all gifts as they arrive.

TWO WEEKS before your wedding:

Check with your newspaper for directions on the wedding announcement, then prepare it accordingly.

Make an appointment with your hairdresser for your wedding hairstyle.

Go with your fiancé for the marriage license.

Complete your trousseau purchases, including any luggage needed for the honeymoon.

Arrange transportation of the bridal party to the ceremony; a limousine is customary for the bride; private cars may be used for other members of the group.

Discuss details of the wedding and reception with your candid photographer.

Check on the delivery of all purchases for your new home.

Arrange to change your name, if you will be doing so, on insurance, bank, employee forms, etc. (If you are keeping your own name, simply plan on continuing to use it.)

Deliver your wedding announcement and photograph to the newspapers.

ONE WEEK before your wedding:

Begin your honeymoon packing.

Make sure announcements are ready to mail on wedding day.

Give or go to the bridesmaids' party.

Arrange the wedding rehearsal and see that each member of the wedding party is informed of the date, time, and place.

Present gifts to your attendants at the bridesmaids' party or rehearsal dinner.

Give a final estimate of the number of reception guests to the caterer.

Check on final details with the florist, photographer, musicians, etc.

Arrange to move your wedding gifts and personal belongings to your new home.

Keep up with your thank-you notes.

Groom's Reminder List

The groom traditionally has fewer official wedding responsibilities than the bride, which leaves him free to handle many of the unexpected things that inevitably come up or the bride cannot fit smoothly into her schedule. The following list spans a six-month period, and should be adjusted if the wedding will take longer to plan.

SIX MONTHS before the wedding:

Order your bride's engagement and wedding rings.

If you'll be sharing wedding expenses, discuss this with your
    fiancée and all the parents involved.

Start making out your guest list.

Arrange a visit with the person who will be performing the cere-
    mony.

Talk over with your fiancée how many ushers you'll need (about
    one for every fifty guests), and begin to select them.

Discuss honeymoon plans with your fiancée and start making
    transportation and accommodation reservations.

If you will be traveling abroad, be sure to update your passport,
    arrange for visas, and check on inoculations.

THREE MONTHS before the wedding:

Complete your family's guest list and give it to your fiancée,
    seeing that all addresses are complete and include zip codes.

Consult with your fiancée about the appropriate suits for you and
    all the men in the wedding to wear; order your wedding at-
    tire.

Decide on whom you want as your best man and ushers and in-
    vite them to participate.

Talk with the male attendants about their wedding attire.

Complete your honeymoon plans and purchase tickets.

Decide with your fiancée who will be responsible for the bride's
    bouquet and going-away corsage; check with her too on
    boutonnières for men in the wedding party and mothers'
    corsages.

ONE MONTH before the wedding:

Pick up the bride's wedding ring, checking the engraving care-
    fully.

Arrange lodging for relatives and ushers from out of town.

Help plan the rehearsal dinner if your parents will be hosting it.

Select a gift for your bride.

Choose gifts for your attendants.

Make sure necessary documents—legal, medical, and religious— are all in order.

See that the ushers have ordered their attire.

TWO WEEKS before the wedding:

Make a date with your fiancée to get the marriage license. (This is the time to celebrate with a special date.)

Check on arrangements for the bachelor dinner, if you will be giving it.

Arrange with your best man for transportation from the reception site to the airport—or wherever you are planning to leave for your honeymoon destination.

Double-check all honeymoon reservations.

ONE WEEK before the wedding:

Present gifts to your attendants, at the bachelors' party, perhaps.

Remind your best man and ushers of the rehearsal time and place, and fill them in on rehearsal dinner details.

Explain any special seating arrangements to the head usher.

Put the clergy's fee in a sealed envelope and give it to the best man —or give him the judge's gift. (In either case, the best man will deliver it.)

Get your going-away clothes ready so you can change after the reception.

Pack for your honeymoon.

Arrange to move belongings to your new home.

Cooperative Planning

Working with others to create a ceremony and reception that will be well-remembered by all is one of the major responsibilities of everyone involved. Yet disagreements such as whether the menu should be lobster or prime rib, whether the bride's limousine should be black or white, whether the invitations should be printed in block letters or script are bound to arise. Some disputes can be solved simply by looking up the answer among the pages in this book. Even so, etiquette is seldom a matter of "right and wrong." The point is that the majority feel comfortable and happy. So if the book says one thing, and most of you would rather do another, choose what's "right" for you.

How to handle those situations when you can't agree? If you spend a little time to get to the bottom of the real issue, you'll often find a way to satisfy everyone's wishes at the same time. Take the mother who insists on a church wedding, while the daughter cries for a ceremony on the lawns of a country inn miles away. The daughter may be shy of crowds, not the faith in which she was raised. The mother may think the out-of-doors very pretty but not worth the long drive. Then why not an intimate chapel service with a reception in the church courtyard or the family's own backyard? Incidentally, simply keeping others—particularly the groom's family—informed of what's going on rather than leaving them out might be all you have to do to assure good feelings about each decision. And asking yourself, "What difference will this make in ten years?" can help put your own preferences in   perspective.

In the end, parents will do well to remember that no matter who pays the bills, it is the bride's and groom's wedding; and the couple should consider that the best thing for their marriage is to get relationships on all sides off to a warm and loving start.

5
Your Invitations and Announcements

Tradition has established guidelines for the wording, the paper, and the engraving or printing of wedding invitations and announcements. At the same time, many informal and original variations are now popular. Which is right for you? Think a moment about your wedding style. For a very formal wedding, the richness of a thick, creamy paper and "the honour of your presence" may seem most suitable. For a less formal celebration, parchment embellished in pastels, perhaps carrying your favorite Bible verse, may appeal to you. The only thing that matters is that your guests receive your message with as much warmth and happiness as you have sent it.

The Guest List

After you and your family have settled on a budget and decided how many guests you wish to invite, ask your fiancé and his family to make up their list, letting them know how many guests you hope they will invite. Usually each family invites half the guests. Sometimes, however, one family will have a longer list— for instance, when only the groom's father and mother, brothers and sisters will be traveling to the bride's home city for the wedding. Another convenient way to divide the guest list is in thirds —the bride's parents provide one-third of the names; the groom's parents, one-third; the couple, one-third. Duplicates on the lists, and, eventually, regrets offer the opportunity to invite people who just had to be eliminated the first time around. Mailing an invitation up to two and a half weeks before the wedding is perfectly acceptable, and that uncle downstate or former classmate away in graduate school will enjoy the invitation whenever it arrives. Incidentally, you may ask not only for names from your fiancé's family, but complete addresses plus zip codes. If your fiancé's parents are divorced, the parent who raised him helps him draw up the list. But he should make sure that everyone to whom the wedding is important is invited—particularly his grandparents.

Do send invitations to your wedding official (and spouse), your fiancé's immediate family, the members of your wedding party and their parents (if you can), even though they've been invited informally. You need not invite companions for single friends on your list—the wedding may be a lot more interesting for everyone if unmarried people come without dates and mingle with one another! But if you wish to invite the friend or fiancé of a single guest, ask for the person's name and address and send a separate invitation (unless the couple live together, in which case you may mail a joint invitation, just as you would do to a married couple).

At the same time you draw up your invitation list, you should also put together your announcement list, including all those acquaintances with whom you wish to share the good news of your marriage. By all means send an invitation to everyone you would like to have with you, even those you are sure will not be able to attend if you won't be sending announcements. Old address and telephone books, alumni directories, Christmas card lists, and club rosters are all helpful in making sure no one is forgotten. And, since neither an invitation nor an announcement requires a gift, you may send them to everyone who will want to share your happiness.

Your fiancé's mother should receive three or four unsealed invitations—wedding mementos—as soon as they are ready. These may be accompanied by a note from you or your mother telling her when the others will be mailed.

Paper and Printing

While handwritten invitations may be sent for a small ceremony of fifty or fewer guests, for a larger wedding you'll undoubtedly want invitations done by your stationer. Traditionally, these are engraved using a special process that "cuts" the letters into the paper. Today, however, less expensive printing processes may take the place of engraving. Your printer or stationer can advise you and show you samples from which to select.

A classic, formal invitation is printed or engraved on the top page of a folded sheet of white or off-white paper and comes with two envelopes. The inner envelope, ungummed and unsealed, encloses the invitation or announcement; the outer one is addressed and stamped.

The typeface you use is largely a matter of personal taste, but here are some examples of traditional looks:

Florentine Script

Venetian Script

Linear Modified Roman

Shaded Roman

Shaded Antique Roman

Park Avenue

Stuyvesant Script

Riviera Script

Of course, you may personalize your invitations and announcements as you wish, choosing translucent or shiny paper, a colored ink, even a border trim or a photograph of you and your groom.

Whatever look you have in mind for your invitations and announcements, you can order from a printer, a jeweler, a stationery or department store, or a bridal salon. Do so at least three months before the ceremony to allow plenty of time for printing, addressing, and mailing. Have the envelopes sent to you in advance (including some extras in case of mistakes). That way they'll be all addressed and ready to mail when the invitations arrive.

Addressing

Make up a master list (if you put it on index cards, you'll have no trouble alphabetizing and eliminating duplications), seeing to it that all names and titles are spelled correctly. Address all invitations by hand in blue, blue-black, or black ink, never by typewriter. You may do the work yourself, ask your bridesmaids or fiancé and families for help, or hire a secretarial service or specialist in calligraphy.

The outside envelope, the one to be sealed and stamped, is addressed to a married couple like this:

Mr. and Mrs. James Wallace McDermott
1088 Fielding Avenue
Metropolis, Ohio 12345

To a single person:

Miss Lucene Bedrosian
407 Kingsley Street, Apartment 4-B
Metropolis, Ohio 12345

The only abbreviations used are *Mr., Mrs., Ms.* (if it is preferred), *Jr.,* and *Dr.* Most elected officials are addressed as *The Honorable* (a judge, for instance); most clergy as *The Reverend* or *The Reverend Father* or *Rabbi;* and high-ranking military personnel as *Commander, Colonel,* etc. Divorcées are either the very traditional *Mrs. Phillips Ross* (a combination of maiden and married surnames) or *Mrs. Joan Ross;* widows, *Mrs. Earl Johnson.* Try to avoid nicknames or initials. Write out streets, cities, and states in full as well. And don't forget zip codes!

New situations may call for new forms of address. Once all women who were doctors, officers in the military, or the like went by their married names for social purposes. Now, some prefer their professional names and titles. Other wives may have retained their maiden names. In these cases, you may send one invitation to both husband and wife, putting her name above his on the envelope, as:

> *Dr. Sheila Vincente*
> *Mr. David Vincente*
> *1010 Maplewood Road*
> *Metropolis, Ohio 12345*

An unmarried couple who live together may receive a joint invitation also:

> *Ms. Jane Adams*
> *Mr. John Snyder*
> *393 Atlantic Boulevard, Apartment 6-F*
> *Metropolis, Ohio 12345*

The unsealed, inner envelope does not include first names or addresses, but reads simply:

> *Mr. and Mrs. McDermott*

or

> *Dr. Vincente and Mr. Vincente*

or

> *Ms. Adams and Mr. Snyder*

If several members of a family are to be invited, avoid using the phrase "and family." Instead, on the inner envelope only, include the name of each child invited, as:

Mr. and Mrs. McDermott
Elaine and Charles

Adult members of a family—everyone over eighteen—should receive separate invitations, whether they still live with their parents or not. You may, however, send one joint invitation to two brothers or sisters living at the same address. Two unrelated friends living together as roommates should each receive their own invitation.

Mailing

The larger, more formal invitation is first folded across the middle of the engraved double sheet, then slipped into the inner envelope with the folded side down. On opening, the guest should first see the names of the wedding sponsors—usually the bride's parents. The less formal, and more popular, invitation is not folded again, but is placed in the envelope as is, with the engraved side facing up.

Extra enclosures—pew cards, reception cards, at-home cards—may be placed next to the engraving or be inserted in one fold of the invitation or announcement. Tissues placed over the lettering to prevent smudging while the ink dries are usually tossed away, but may be left in place for convenience. However, if they are not inserted by the printer, there is no need to add them.

The unsealed inner envelope is placed in the outer envelope so that the guest's name immediately comes to view when the outside envelope is opened.

Mail invitations four to six weeks before the wedding; two months ahead is courteous if you will marry during the holiday season, when friends and relatives will be juggling many commitments on their calendars.

Do allow people time to consider your invitation and to word their replies. Depending on the formality of your invitation, they will respond with formal written acceptances or regrets, with informal notes, even phone calls or response cards (if you've chosen to send them). It's two weeks until the wedding, and you still haven't heard? Then a member of your family may call and check: "We are all looking forward to seeing you at Rachel's wedding the twenty-third, Mr. Goldberg, will you be able to join us?" When each invitation is accounted for, tell your caterer how many guests to expect.

Formal announcements—as beautiful as classic invitations—sent to those who will not be asked to the wedding should be mailed the day of the wedding or immediately afterward. Do include a return address on invitations and announcements both. Once it was permissible to emboss the return address colorlessly on the envelope flap. Now, however, the U.S. Post Office requires that all return addresses appear in the upper left-hand corner of the envelope.

Wording Your Invitations

Parents of the bride usually issue the invitations and announcements, whether or not she still shares their home. If your parents are no longer living, your guardian, closest relatives, or family friends may sponsor your wedding and issue the invitations. If your parents are divorced, the one who raised you customarily issues the invitations and announcements. Are you confused about the wording? It helps to remember that the names at the top of a wedding invitation refer to who is sponsoring the wedding, not to who is paying for it. Even if you and your fiancé will be paying, your parents can still be considered sponsors and should feel proud to see their names on the first line.

On formal invitations, all names are spelled out in full without nicknames. Spell out numbers, including those in short addresses, and *Junior,* if space permits. The date is written, *Saturday the sixth of July,* with the year spelled out on the following line. You may omit the year from invitations. The time is indicated as *four o'clock* or *half after four o'clock.* If there are churches with similar names in the same city, and many of your guests are unfamiliar with the location, the street address should be indicated beneath the name of the ceremony site. The state may or may not be included, depending, again, on how many of your guests are familiar with the area.

The honour of your presence is always requested for a religious ceremony, but *the pleasure of your company* is asked for the reception. You may bid a reply to a reception invitation with *R.S.V.P., Please respond, Kindly respond,* or *The favour of a reply is requested. Honour* and *favour* are always spelled with a *u.*

When the bride's family is sponsoring the wedding, the typical invitation   reads:

> *Mr. and Mrs. Charles Andrew Jones*
> *request the honour of your presence*
> *at the marriage of their daughter*
> *Mary Lynn*
> *to*
> *Mr. Edward Robins Hill*
> *Saturday, the sixth of May*
> *at four o'clock*
> *All Saints' Church*
> *Barton, Texas*

The formal reception card to accompany this invitation would read:

> *Mr. and Mrs. Charles Andrew Jones*
> *request the pleasure of your company*
> *Saturday, the sixth of May*
> *at half after four o'clock*
> *Glenn Oaks Country Club*

R.S.V.P.
Sixty-two Laurel Lane
Barton, Texas 12345

The reception card may also take this simplified form:

Reception
immediately following the ceremony
Glen Oaks Country Club

Kindly respond
Sixty-two Laurel Lane
Barton, Texas 12345

Frequently, the groom's parents' names also appear on the invitation, as an honor, whether they are cosponsoring the ceremony or not. The invitation would then read:

Mr. and Mrs. Charles Andrew Jones
request the honour of your presence
at the marriage of their daughter
Mary Lynn
to
Mr. Edward Robins Hill
son of
Mr. and Mrs. Donald Lawrence Hill
Saturday, the sixth of May
at four o'clock
All Saints' Church
Barton, Texas

If the reception has a larger guest list than the ceremony, invitations are issued to the reception with ceremony cards enclosed. The invitation reads:

Mr. and Mrs. Charles Andrew Jones
request the pleasure of your company
at the wedding reception of their daughter
Mary Lynn
and
Mr. Edward Robins Hill
Saturday, the sixth of May
at half after four o'clock
Glen Oaks Country Club
Barton, Texas

Please respond
Sixty-two Laurel Lane
Barton, Texas 12345

The ceremony card reads:

Mr. and Mrs. Charles Andrew Jones
request the honour of your presence
Saturday, the sixth of May
at four o'clock
All Saints' Church
Barton, Texas

The ceremony card may also take this simplified form:

Ceremony
at four o'clock
All Saints' Church

A similar reception invitation that includes the names of the groom's parents might read:

Mr. and Mrs. Charles Andrew Jones
request the pleasure of your company
at the wedding reception of their daughter
Mary Lynn
and
Mr. Edward Robins Hill
son of
Mr. and Mrs. Donald Lawrence Hill
Saturday, the sixth of May
etc.

Another form for the longer reception invitation which indicates joint sponsorship is common. However, it does not spell out the relationships of parents to the bride and groom quite so clearly. And some couples may not be comfortable with the word "children." Others may think the wording has a particularly warm sound. The invitation reads:

Mr. and Mrs. Charles Andrew Jones
and
Mr. and Mrs. Donald Lawrence Hill
request the pleasure of your company
at the wedding reception of their children
Mary Lynn
and
Edward Robins
Saturday, the sixth of May
etc.

Should there be too few guests invited to the ceremony to warrant special cards, tuck in a plain or printed informal note card with the simple, handwritten message, "Ceremony at four o'clock, All Saints' Church."

If all guests are to be invited to both the ceremony and a reception that takes place right after, a combined invitation may be sent without separate enclosure cards. This very popular form reads:

> *Mr. and Mrs. Charles Andrew Jones*
> *request the honour of your presence*
> *at the marriage of their daughter*
> *Mary Lynn*
> *to*
> *Mr. Edward Robins Hill*
> *Saturday, the sixth of May*
> *at four o'clock*
> *All Saints' Church*
> *Barton, Texas*
> *and afterwards at*
> *Glen Oaks Country Club*

Please respond
Sixty-two Laurel Lane
Barton, Texas 12345

To include both sets of parents, follow the form shown earlier in this chapter.

For a small, informal wedding, printed invitations are not necessary. Instead, your parents may send handwritten notes, or they may invite guests personally at least two weeks before the ceremony. Such a note might read:

Dear Rose,
Judith and Michael are to be married at half past three on Sunday, the fifth of September, in the chapel of Temple Emanuel here in Green Heights. It will be a small wedding with a reception afterward at our house. You know how much we all want you to be with us on that day.

Affectionately,
Ruth

It is more gracious to write notes, but it is all right, too, for you or your parents to telephone your invitations. If you make the call, you might say, "Mother and Dad want me to invite you. . ." so that guests know your family is hosting the wedding.

Special Invitations

Widowed parents: If one of your parents has died, the wedding invitation takes the following form, unless the widow or widower has remarried. A widow would send an invitation reading:

Mrs. Robert Kowolsky
requests the honour of your presence
at the marriage of her daughter
Theresa Louise
etc.

A widower would substitute the phrase, *his daughter.*
When the bride's mother has remarried, the following wording is used:

Mr. and Mrs. Ricardo Rojas
request the honour of your presence
at the marriage of Mrs. Rojas's daughter
(or, if the bride is close to her stepfather,
their daughter)
Angela Madelena Mendoza
etc.

When a remarried father sponsors the wedding, this wording is used:

Mr. and Mrs. Victor Mendoza
request the honour of your presence
at the marriage of Mr. Mendoza's daughter
(or, if the bride is close to her stepmother,
their daughter)
Angela   Madelena
etc.

Divorced parents: When the parents of the bride are divorced, the wedding invitation is usually issued by the parent who raised the bride. If she or he has remarried, the invitation would be worded just as for widowed parents who've remarried, above.

If your mother issues the invitations, and she has not remarried, she may use either the traditional divorcée's combination of her maiden and married surnames, as "Mrs. Collins Anderson," or drop the "Mrs." altogether and simply use "Sarah Collins Anderson." If she ordinarily goes by her first, middle, and married surname (Mrs. Sarah Beth Anderson), that, too, is now considered acceptable. The rest of the invitation is worded as for a widowed   parent.

If your divorced father is sponsoring the wedding, then the invitation carries his full name and the phrase, "his daughter."

When divorced parents are still very friendly, they may wish to send a joint invitation to their daughter's wedding. Generally they avoid "Mr. and Mrs." since that is no longer the case, and list their names—remarried or not—separately, as:

Sarah   Collins   Anderson
and
Steven   Randolph   Anderson
request the honour of your presence
at the marriage of their daughter
Abigail Blake
to

Christopher Howard Geist
etc.

Notice in this case that the "Mr." can also be omitted from the groom's name to keep the look of the invitation consistent.

Sometimes the daughter of divorced parents would like both to be acknowledged equally at her wedding, but they are not entirely comfortable with their names appearing together. Then the solution might be for one parent to issue the wedding invitations and the other the reception invitations—mailed in the same outer envelope, of course.

Is your groom the one with divorced parents? The same guidelines apply, and the samples here can be adapted accordingly.

Sponsors other than parents of the bride: If the bride is being sponsored by other relatives, words like "his sister," "her sister," "his," "her," or "their niece" are substituted for the phrase "their daughter" to indicate the relationship. Close friends may also sponsor the bride. Then the invitation gives the bride's full name, with "Miss" before it:

Mr. and Mrs. George Anthony Donato
request the honour of your presence
at the marriage of
Miss Cheryl Diane Callas
to
Mr. Arnold Lee Gregory
etc.

Sponsorship by the couple themselves: When the bride has no sponsor—no family or close friends nearby—and she and her fiancé have been on their own for a while—they may prefer to issue their own invitations. Such an invitation reads:

*The honour of your presence
is requested at the marriage of
Miss Margaret Jean Murphy
to
Mr. Leo Stanley Stark
Saturday, the fifth of November
at eleven o'clock
St. Cecilia's Church
South Bay, California*

The invitation might include the simplified reception card shown earlier in this chapter, or a card saying:

*The pleasure of your company is requested
Saturday, the fifth of November
at half after eleven o'clock
The Waterside
South Bay, California*

*R.S.V.P.
1600 Ocean Parkway, Apartment 12-L
South Bay, California 12345*

Second marriages: Whether the bride has been widowed or divorced, formal invitations to her wedding may be issued. Her wedding may be hosted by those close to her or by her and her fiancé themselves. There are lovely options in wording (see them in Chapter 11).

Double weddings: Most often a double wedding involves two sisters. The invitation to the occasion would read:

*Mr. and Mrs. Nicholas Pappas
request the honour of your presence
at the marriage of their daughters
Katherine Denise
to*

Mr. Milton Zara
and
Christine Eugenia
to
Mr. Matthew Hercules
at half after seven o'clock, the first of August
St. Barbara Greek Orthodox Church
Inport, Connecticut

When the brides are not sisters, separate invitations may be sent by each family, or they may mail a joint invitation:

Mr. and Mrs. Samuel Catt Saulsberry
and
Mr. and Mrs. Gaylord Rogers
request the honour of your presence
at the marriage of their daughters
Stephanie Caroline Saulsberry
to
Mr. Bruce Raymond Harnett
and
Brenda Lou Rogers
to
Mr. Randolph Sloan Lincoln
etc.

Personalized invitations: Couples and their parents today, especially those who wish to share religious feelings with their guests, may choose to send invitations worded in other than the classic manner. An experienced printer can suggest complementary paper—a scroll of parchment, perhaps, or a prettily decorated pastel. Or, of course, the invitations may be written by hand. If composing your own wording, do remember to include the basics that are so frequently forgotten on personalized invitations: sponsor's names; ceremony site, date, time; reception site, date, time; address, if any, for replies. Just so long as your invitation is easy for guests to follow, you may adapt any traditional guidelines as you see fit (for instance, substituting numerals for complete   spellings).

As with any touch used to personalize a wedding, some guests may comment. It is likely that this will be minimal if you take care to make the invitation warm but not effusive, concise rather than quite long, and in keeping with the mood of the entire celebration —less than ultraformal. One invitation to a semiformal wedding:

Warner and Pamela Simpson
and
William and Mary Marcus
invite you
to share in the joy
of the marriage
uniting our children
Nicole and Jerry
at the First Baptist Church
607 Lincoln Avenue
New   Petersburg
Saturday, the 30th of August, 1981
at 4 P.M.
Worship with us, witness their vows
and
join us afterward in
the Church Fellowship Hall.
If you are unable to attend, we ask your
presence in thought and in prayer.

Special Enclosures

At-home cards: At-home cards may be enclosed with formal invitations but are more often used with announcements (see the section later in this chapter). What are they? Small cards that let everyone know the couple's address and the date they will be ready to receive mail—and visitors—there. A typical at-home card reads:

At home
after the twenty-sixth of August
1413 Fountain Avenue
Atlanta, Georgia, 12345

When enclosed with announcements, they may also take this form:

Mr. and Mrs. John Simon Eagle
after the tenth of April
1035 Fifth Avenue, Apartment 9-B
New York, New York 12345

If the bride plans to retain her maiden or professional name, the at-home card is the perfect place to announce that, as:

Dr. Mary Ann Janacek
Mr. John Simon Eagle
after the tenth of April
etc.

Ceremony cards: When there is any chance that uninvited persons may try to attend the ceremony, engraved cards may be enclosed with invitations to be presented at the door for admittance. These are used only for a very formal wedding, usually of celebrities—like screen stars or politicians—and read:

Please present this card
The First Congregational Church
Saturday, the twelfth of March

Pew cards: Special seating arrangements for relatives and for
very close friends are indicated with these cards. They are best
sent after the acceptance has been received to ensure the correct
number of reserved seats. But they, too, may be enclosed with the
invitation. There are several forms, the simplest being a handwritten note from the bride's parents. A more elaborate form
reads:

Please present this card
The First Congregational Church
Saturday, the twelfth of March
Pew number 9

General reservations may also be indicated by the phrase
"within the ribbons"—in which case pretty satin ribbons or bows
decorate the last pew of the reserved section, and all special guests
are escorted to seats in front of this pew. The phrase may appear
on either of the first two cards above in place of the special pew
number. However, general reservations are used only for very
large, very formal wedding.

Reception response cards: To send them or not is a question to
consider carefully. Traditionally they are avoided. But reception
response cards are gaining acceptability in many areas and may
be enclosed with invitations, as long as this is welcomed as a convenience among the majority of your guests. Others look forward
to observing the courteous custom of a personal reply. It is up to
you to decide. If you do enclose response cards, the return envelopes should already be stamped and addressed. The following
form seems to be the clearest and easiest for guests:

Miss Lorraine Doyle

accepts

regrets

Saturday, July second

Court Hotel

Charlottesville

Maps: are seldom enclosed in formal invitations. Usually any guest requiring directions to the ceremony site will ask for them at the time of response. After the ceremony, ushers take on the responsibility of seeing that guests get instructions to the reception. However, in the event that it would be most helpful to receive maps along with the invitations, then the maps should be drawn and printed in as beautiful and professional a manner as the invitation itself. (Be prepared with extras, in case guests misplace theirs.)

Military and Other Titles

Traditionally, the bride's last name and title of "Miss," "Ms.," or "Mrs." (for certain second-time brides) are omitted on the formal invitation, while the groom's full name, preceded by "Mr." is used. Perhaps, though, the bride and groom wish their names to be in the same form. In this case, they may leave off titles and both use their first, middle, and last names.

If the bride's father, the groom, or the groom's father (when his name appears on the invitation) are clergymen, physicians, high elected officials, or members of the armed forces on active duty, they may go by their professional titles. A clergyman's full title— The Reverend, Bishop, Rabbi—is spelled out before his name. The name of a medical doctor is preceded by "Dr." instead of "Mr." When the bride or her mother is a physician or member of the clergy, the title has customarily been dropped, although it now may be included along with her complete name. The titles of senators and judges, and other high officials, may be used, but those of lesser officials are usually omitted.

Military titles and social invitations are subject to changing regulations and should always be verified with the commanding officer. Even so, the title of the bride's father is usually spelled out before his name. The groom's title appears before his name only if he holds a rank equivalent to or higher than captain in the Army or commander in the Navy. If he occupies a lesser rank, it may be listed with his branch of service, as follows:

Jeffrey Ronald Sherman
Lieutenant, United States Army

If the groom is an enlisted man, his branch of service may be shown without mention of his rank. In either case, the title "Mr." is omitted. Reserve officers do not use military titles unless they are on active duty. A bride in the military service follows the same guidelines as the groom—or she may do without her title in favor of the familiar first-name form.

Recalling Invitations

If a formal wedding is postponed or cancelled after the invitations have gone out, all invited guests must be notified as soon as possible. When time permits, this is best done with printed cards, rush-ordered from the stationer. If there has been a death in the family, the card would read:

Mrs. Gerald Timothy Allen
regrets that the death of
Mr. Allen
obliges her to recall the invitations
to the wedding of her daughter
Saturday, the third of February

An invitation recalled in this manner indicates only that the wedding will not take place as originally planned. When a death or serious illness in the family means a large wedding would be inappropriate, the marriage may still take place as a small family ceremony. The couple may wear their formal wedding attire, but they usually have honor attendants only.

If the wedding is postponed and a new date set, you may send a new printed invitation to your guests. Such a notification would read:

Mr. and Mrs. Stuart Dean Jefferson
announce that the marriage of their daughter
Virginia
to
Mr. Frank Martin Gallagher
has been postponed from
Saturday, the fourth of October
until
Saturday, the eighteenth of October
at four o'clock
Grace Episcopal Church
Wilfordshire

If the wedding is cancelled, invitations should be promptly recalled with an engraved or printed card reading:

Mr. and Mrs. Warren Troy Peterson
announce that the marriage of
their daughter
Ellen
to
Henry Karl Schneider
will not take place

If time is short, invitations may be recalled by personal notes, telegrams, or telephone calls. Notes should be patterned after the cards, and signed by the person who issued the invitations. Calls should be made in the name of the bride's parents. Reasons other than a death or illness in the family are not usually mentioned.

How to Word Your Announcements

Announcements are problem-solvers. Never mailed to anyone who has been invited to the wedding, they can go out after an intimate ceremony for family only, an elopement, a wedding so far away many people could not attend. Business associates with whom the couple work day-to-day might also receive announcements. (Remember, no one on the announcement list need feel obliged to send you a gift.) With time and budget on the minds of more and more couples and parents, sending announcements is an old wedding custom that makes sense today.

Printing and paper for announcements are the same as for invitations. Announcements should be addressed just as wedding invitations are and, whenever possible, mailed out immediately after the ceremony. A typical announcement reads:

Mr. and Mrs. Peter Young Chow
have the honour of announcing
the marriage of their daughter
Annette   Elizabeth
and
Mr. Leonard Park Ling
on Friday, the tenth of July
one thousand nine hundred and eighty-two
Our Redeemer Lutheran Church
Seattle,   Washington

The bride's parents may also "have the honour to announce the marriage" or simply "announce the marriage." The date, year, and city in which the marriage took place are always included. It is optional, however, to mention the actual ceremony site.

When the bride or her parents are divorced or widowed, the wording is varied in the same way as it is for invitations. If you have no parents or close relatives to issue the announcements, you and your groom may issue your own. This is also an option for mature couples or those who have been previously married. Such an announcement would read:

Miss Deborah Schwartz
(or, Deborah Suzanne Schwartz, Mrs. Meyer Schwartz, Dr. Deborah Schwartz, etc.)
and
Mr. Eric Davis Fisher
announce their marriage
Friday, the twenty-seventh of November
One thousand nine hundred and eighty-one
Chicago, Illinois

Post-Wedding Parties

Occasionally someone will host a party for the newlywed couple after the wedding has occurred. Complete with receiving line and formal dress, the party will call for invitations that are equally formal. Such an occasion would be when the groom's grandparents want everyone in their hometown to see their grandson grown and married and to meet his wife. It might not be a time for gift-giving but for good wishes. And the invitation would read:

Mr. and Mrs. Albert Hughes Hudson
request the pleasure of your company
at a reception in honour of
Mr. and Mrs. Theodore Russell Hudson
Sunday, the fourteenth of January
at four o'clock
Castle Mountain Inn
Woodtown, Vermont

R.S.V.P.
263 Spruce Road
Woodtown, Vermont 12345

If the party is almost like a second wedding reception, hosted by parents of the couple or the couple themselves for close friends and relatives in another part of the country, reception cards like those shown earlier in the chapter may be enclosed with announcements. Or formal reception invitations, if it's a very large party, may be sent. Handwritten notes are always appropriate.

Reaffirmation of Vows

Whether they have eloped, married in city hall, or come to the point of celebrating a very special wedding anniversary, many couples are asking others to witness a ceremony where they will speak their marriage vows once again. A service will be designed with them by the official involved, and could take place in a house of worship or at home. A possible invitation for this ceremony:

The honour of your presence
is requested at the reaffirmation
of the wedding vows of

Mr. and Mrs. Walter Aldrich VerderMay
Saturday, the eighth of June
at three o'clock
Christian Reformed Church
Amsterdam, Michigan
and afterward at
a reception in
the church parlour

Wedding Anniversaries

If it is to be a formal celebration for more than fifty, formal invitations are appropriate. Typical would be a party given by a daughter and her husband for her parents. The invitation could say:

Mr. and Mrs. Joshua Speigel
request the pleasure of your company
at a reception to honour
the thirtieth wedding anniversary
of her parents
Mr. and Mrs. Morris Weidman
the evening of Wednesday, the second of August
half after eight o'clock
1614 Greatfalls Avenue
Minneapolis, Minnesota 12345
Kindly reply

Whenever debating between one wording for an invitation or announcement and another, remember that a name is very special, very important to a person. What makes everyone mentioned happy will surely be an invitation issued in the spirit of your wedding.

6
The Wedding Party

A wedding is as much for family and friends as for the bride and groom themselves. And a wedding party is aptly named. After all, the people you invite to be your attendants—the pal from your fiancé's old neighborhood to the new friend who'll soon be your sister-in-law—are people who will make your wedding the best party of your lives.

The Bride

You have a great many things to do before that very special day. The ultimate responsibility for everyone's comfort and for a smoothly run event is yours. After discussing budget with your family (and with your groom's, perhaps), you and he will be able to decide how elaborate a wedding and reception you'll have, and where it will all take place. Once the decisions have been made and you make them known, parents, relatives, friends, and co-workers will begin volunteering to handle some of the tasks, and of course, you will delegate others. But it will still be up to you to see that the plans are carried out.

One of the most pleasant privileges of being a bride is choosing your attendants. It is also your prerogative to find the dresses they will wear. It is considerate, however, to let them make the final selection from about three styles you like. It's doubly thoughtful to shop with an eye to your maids' budgets, their prospects for wearing their dresses again, and their attractiveness. Your maids will look prettiest when they feel pretty—you'll want the outfit to flatter the former roommate who is still trying to fill out, as much as it does your little sister who is forever on a diet.

To show your appreciation to your attendants, you give each one a small gift—a pendant or silver picture frame, maybe, engraved with her initials and the wedding date—as a memento. You may entertain for your bridesmaids as well, but this is up to you.

Another optional custom you'll probably want to follow is that of exchanging gifts with your groom. Almost anything you know he'd like, from a new tennis racquet to a leather briefcase, would be suitable.

The last (but certainly not least) of your responsibilities is the acknowledging of your wedding gifts. You must write a personal note of appreciation for each and every gift you receive. Your groom might help, especially if presents come to the wedding addressed to you both or arrive from people only he knows. The notes need not be long, but they should be prompt and sincere. The best policy is to write a few each day so that you won't get behind, and so the message to the uncle who sent the savings bond is as fresh and meaningful as the thanks to the neighbor who carried over the china sugar bowl. (For more details on thank-you notes, see Chapter 16.)

Even if you are working or going to school full time, you can prepare in a way that will leave you relaxed and able to enjoy your wedding day, and ready to dash off on your honeymoon with a carefree good-bye.

The Groom

Your groom's first responsibility is to see that his family's guest list is compiled, with no more names on it than you and your family have agreed upon. He may compare the services of caterers, photographers, and other professionals with you, and you will visit the ceremony official together. On his own, he is privileged to choose his best man and ushers and may entertain them if he likes. He makes sure his attendants are informed about proper dress for the wedding and presents each of them with a small gift, perhaps an initialed belt buckle or key ring.

You may pick out your wedding ring with him, but your groom buys it and has it engraved, just as you do with the ring he will wear. He may give you a special wedding gift as well. The groom assumes responsibility for getting the marriage license and any other necessary documents, and he makes all the arrangements for the wedding trip.

Throughout the planning months, you will find that he is the person who can handle the details someone else forgot—checking on available hotels for out-of-town guests, finding out how much the musicians charge for overtime.

On wedding day, your groom's primary concern is the proverbial "getting to the church on time," although his best man will have a hand in this as well as everything else. The groom accepts the congratulations of the guests in the receiving line, responds to all toasts, then whisks you away with him for a happy honeymoon.

The Maid or Matron of Honor

Your maid or matron of honor should be someone who is very close to you, perhaps your sister, or a dear friend, favorite cousin, or roommate. You needn't ask your fiancé's sister to be your honor attendant unless she also happens to be especially close.

If you have two sisters or best friends, you may ask both to be honor attendants, dividing the official duties between them. Ask one to hold your bouquet during the ceremony, for example, the other to present you with your groom's ring. Let them decide between themselves who will precede you down the aisle, stand beside your groom in the receiving line, and sit at his left at the bridal table.

The honor attendant has no definite pre-wedding responsibilities, but is expected to assist the bride wherever she can. She might help address the invitations, or take charge of recording and displaying your wedding gifts. When you cry, "Oh, I'll never get it all done!" she's likely to be the one handing you a tissue.

If you have several bridesmaids, your honor attendant might arrange to have their outfits fitted, see that each is dressed perfectly to the last detail, and make certain they're at the church on time. She assembles her own wedding outfit, paying for everything except the flowers. She attends all pre-wedding parties and may give one herself. At a home wedding, the honor attendant may be the person who greets the ceremony official and shows him or her where to change.

The honor attendant is usually one of the two witnesses required by law to sign the marriage certificate. She precedes you and your father down the aisle, arranges your train and veil, and holds your bouquet during the ceremony. She also passes you the groom's ring (for safekeeping up until this point, she may wear it on her middle finger or thumb, or carry it in a hidden pocket or dainty bag). The honor attendant stands next to the groom in the receiving line and sits on his left at the bride's table. Once the receiving line disperses, she is free to enjoy the reception as an honored guest, but she may take time out to help you freshen up now and then, and finally, to change—before she bids you a fond farewell.

The Best Man

This indispensable role is usually filled by the groom's most trustworthy friend or relative. His brother, cousin, best friend, even his father, all are appropriate choices.

The duties of the best man are many and varied. He is chief of staff at the wedding, toastmaster at the reception, and personal aide and advisor to the groom, checking on such things as bills for the flowers, accommodations for out-of-town ushers, along with the groom, if need be. It's the best man's responsibility to see that the groom is properly outfitted and at the church in time for the ceremony, and that the ceremony official is paid (along with any altar boys that should be remembered). The best man takes charge of the marriage license (which he signs as a witness) and the bride's wedding ring, producing each at the proper time. He may also supervise the ushers, making sure that all are uniformly dressed, thoroughly briefed, and at the ceremony site at the appointed hour.

Although the best man does not participate in the receiving line, he does have a number of reception responsibilities. He sits to the right of the bride and proposes the first toast to the new couple, usually a wish for health, happiness, and prosperity. After the toasts, he collects any congratulatory telegrams and reads them aloud if the bride and groom wish. He helps see that the reception goes as it should, and that no practical jokes are played on the couple. . . . The best man is the one that'll make sure, for example, that the windshield of the getaway car isn't so painted up or covered with paper streamers, the driver won't have a safe view.

Another of the best man's duties is to get the newlyweds off on their honeymoon. He helps the groom into his going-away clothes, assists with any last-minute packing. He also takes charge of the luggage, making sure it is locked in the honeymoon car or checked ahead at the station or airport. When you and your groom leave the reception at last, the best man will escort you to your car or drive you off. Then, as you make your departure, he will hand over the keys, tickets, and baggage checks given to him for safekeeping.

The first business day after the wedding, the best man might also see to it that all men's rental clothes are returned to the formal-wear store, and that any gifts of money received at the wedding are deposited in the appropriate bank accounts.

The Bridesmaids

The number of bridesmaids you'll have in your ceremony depends on its size and style, ranging from none at a small, informal wedding to as many as twelve for a large, formal one. Again, it is the bride's prerogative to choose her attendants from among her friends and relatives. Custom has it that they will be close to her age. If you have young sisters or cousins between the ages of nine and fourteen, they may participate as junior bridesmaids (they walk first in the procession, need no partners in the recessional, and have no specific duties). It is nice to ask at least one relative of the groom—his sister or a favorite cousin, perhaps—to be a bridesmaid. Although, traditionally, pregnant women do not participate as attendants, they may if they are certain to feel comfortable throughout the pre-wedding activities and by the time the wedding day arrives.

Bridesmaids have no particular pre-wedding responsibilities. Yet they usually offer to run errands, address envelopes, and help the bride in any way they can. They are invited to all the pre-wedding parties and may give one if they wish. Bridesmaids assemble their own wedding outfits, paying for them as well (although you may assume this expense). Unless you are having all the flowers delivered directly to the ceremony site, they pick up their bouquets at your home an hour or so before the ceremony. Bridesmaids always take part in the wedding procession and usually stand at the bride's side during the ceremony. They may all greet guests in the receiving line or take turns if you prefer. They sit alternately with the ushers at the bride's table. They take part in all the reception festivities and, if unmarried, are usually in the front ranks when the bride tosses her flowers. Incidentally, you may feel free to invite only the woman of a married couple to be in your wedding. And if both husband and wife participate, they need not be paired in the recessional nor be seated side by side at the reception. Mingling and meeting new people is one of the things that makes a wedding so much fun for everybody!

The Ushers

Ushers seat the guests at the ceremony and act as escorts for the bridesmaids. Except for junior bridesmaids, there should be an usher for every bridesmaid in the wedding party, as it's customary for them to walk out together in the recessional. To avoid seating delays, there should also be at least one usher for every fifty guests. Your groom might ask his brothers, future brothers-in-law, cousins, and best friends, married or single, to act in this capacity. He should also include any brothers or close relatives of yours who are adult enough to handle the job.

The ushers usually attend all the pre-wedding parties the groom goes to and may give one if they wish. They provide their own wedding clothes, renting the proper formal attire if they do not own it. Boutonnières are provided by the groom, gloves and neckwear too when these are not included in the rental package. Renting from one source, of course, assures the most coordinated look for the men.

Ushers arrive at the ceremony site forty-five minutes to an hour before the ceremony time, and assemble near the entrance. As the guests arrive, an usher steps forward and offers his right arm to each woman. If she does not present a pew card and he does not know her, he asks if she is a friend of the bride or of the groom, then seats her accordingly. This usually means bride's guests on the left, groom's on the right; the opposite in Jewish services. But when one side has many more guests than the other, the usher may also explain, "We will all be sitting together today," to guarantee everyone will have a clear view. Late-arriving guests are shown to the best available seats on the side with more room.

When a man and a woman arrive together, traditionally the woman takes the usher's arm, and the man follows them down the aisle. What to do if several women appear together? Seat the eldest first. Unless he is elderly and in need of assistance, a man alone may simply be accompanied to his seat by an usher. A new alternative is simply for the usher to lead people to their seats, after saying something like "follow me." All the groomsmen are expected to make polite conversation (in low tones, of course) with guests as they walk unhurriedly down the aisle: "Lovely day for a wedding, isn't it, Mrs. Lane?" "I'm glad you could fly in, Uncle Mort—can't wait to hear the toast you've got in mind this time."

The groom usually designates a head usher to supervise special seating arrangements. If one of the ushers is the brother of the bride or groom, he will probably escort his own mother to her place. Otherwise, the head usher assumes responsibility for the mothers. Should an aisle carpet or pew ribbons be used, the groom appoints two ushers to take care of unrolling them.

Ushers participate in both the procession and the recessional, returning to escort mothers and honored or frail guests from the church first. Next, two ushers loosen the pew ribbons, then pause at the side of each facing pew, signaling guests to file out row by row, from front to back. In addition, the ushers should be prepared to direct guests to parking and rest room facilities as well as to the reception site. They make certain the ceremony site is cleared of all belongings of the wedding party before leaving for the reception themselves.

Ushers do not stand in the receiving line, but they do sit at the bridal table. They often propose toasts to the bride and groom. Throughout most of the reception, however, they simply circulate and make sure that all the guests—especially the bridesmaids—have a wonderful time.

What do you do if, because of illness, a bridesmaid or usher drops out of the wedding party at the last minute? Luckily, this seldom happens. But when it does, you have two choices: find a replacement who fits the outfit and wants to help, even though you could not ask him or her to participate long ago; or go ahead without the original attendant. In either case, do send along flowers and special souvenirs of the wedding to let the person know he or she has been with you in thought on your special day.

Child Attendants

Children can add a great deal of charm to a wedding ceremony.

And if you are marrying a second time, their being a part of the wedding will make them feel that much more a part of your marriage (see Chapter 11). But very young children who are not with you every day or not often dressed up or never in a crowd may behave unpredictably. This is why one or two children between the ages of four and eight may be all the addition you need to the solemnity of your ceremony. If you don't know any children well enough, it may be preferable not to invite them to participate.

The flower girl is the most popular child attendant. She may walk alone, with the ring bearer, or with another flower girl about the same size, but she always comes immediately before the bride in the procession. Traditionally, flower girls carried baskets of loose rose petals to strew in the bride's path. But the possibility of someone slipping on the petals is very real. So today, most flower girls carry a basket of posies, a tiny nosegay, or a flower-covered muff. In any case, see that the girl's flowers are the same front and back so they will look pretty no matter how she holds them.

The ring bearer, who can as easily be a girl as a boy nowadays, balances a white pillow with a fake ring tied to the center with ribbons or stitched down lightly with satin thread. (The best man keeps the bride's real ring tucked safely in his pocket; the honor attendant keeps the groom's real ring slipped on her finger or thumb, or in a special pocket or purse.) After the ceremony, the cushion is turned upside down so the dummy ring doesn't show. Although he or she may be paired with a flower girl, the ring bearer usually walks alone in the procession, immediately preceding the flower girl (if there is one) or the bride.

Pages or trainbearers always come in pairs and are about the same size. They are generally little boys, but girls, too, may serve in this capacity. You will not need pages, of course, unless your dress has a very long train for them to carry.

Young child attendants may attend the rehearsal so they can practice their parts (more than once or twice, though, may not help). They need not go to pre-wedding parties and are often excused from the reception as well. During the ceremony, you may choose to have a child attendant slip in your parents' pew and sit down rather than risk having him or her fidget through the ceremony at the altar.

The Bride's Mother

Your mother helps you compile the guest list, arrange the details of the ceremony and reception, and select your wedding outfit and trousseau, if you like. (It is your choice, not a necessity, that she accompany you to shop for your dress, and go along when you and your groom select items for your household.) Your mother may also keep track of your gifts, seeing that they are attractively displayed in a safe spot. It's your mother's responsibility to keep your father and the groom's parents posted on the progress of the wedding plans. She should inform your fiancé's mother of her choice on wedding attire so that their dresses will be of the same length and accessorized in the same way.

If you will be traveling to your parents' hometown just for the wedding, you are probably counting on your mother to do most of the on-site planning—budget in two identical wedding notebooks and plenty of long distance phone calls to stay in touch.

Your mother is the official hostess for your wedding. She is privileged to sit in the very first pew on the bride's side of the aisle. She is the last person to be escorted to her seat before the wedding and the first to be ushered out after it is over. As hostess for the reception, she greets all the guests at the head of the receiving line and sits in the place of honor at the parents' table.

The Bride's Father

Your father rides to the ceremony with you in the limousine and escorts you down the aisle. After giving you away (if you will observe this tradition), he joins your mother in the first row. As the official host of the reception, he usually mingles with the guests, getting the party going, instead of standing in the receiving line. He's the last person to leave the reception, and the one who bids the guests good-bye.

When you are ready to leave the reception, you should take a few moments alone with both your mother and father for a hug, a kiss, and "thank you for all you've done."

Since your father's part is a prominent one, it is important that his attire blend with that of your groom and the other men in the wedding party.

If your father is not living, you may ask your brother, uncle or other male relative, a close family friend, or an usher to escort you down the aisle. Your mother may do so, if she is comfortable. In any case, she would then give you away.

Your parents are divorced? Your father may still escort you down the aisle and give you away. Instead of sitting in the first pew with your mother, however, he would sit in the third row on the bride's side of the aisle.

The Groom's Parents

Although the role played by the groom's parents is smaller than that of your parents, they should be treated with equal respect. Your fiancé's mother should be invited to all the showers, and both of his parents should be included in the rehearsal dinner if they will not be giving it themselves. Your fiancé's parents contribute to the guest list for the wedding and reception, and may or may not offer to share expenses. They consult with your parents on the proper wedding attire and dress accordingly. The groom's parents are honored guests at the ceremony and are seated, just before your mother, in the first pew on the groom's side of the aisle. The groom's mother always stands in the receiving line to meet the guests, but his father's participation is optional. Before you leave the reception, your groom will want a few quiet minutes with his parents, just as you have had.

Special Members of the Wedding

If your wedding party is not large enough to include all of your favorite relatives and friends, or if you have brothers and sisters who are not old enough to participate as attendants, you may include them in other ways. Young girls or boys, for example, might distribute Mass books or *yarmulkes,* give out wedding programs, or serve as acolytes at the ceremony; at the reception, they might take charge of the guest book, pass out packets of rice or groom's cake, or help with refreshments.

Occasionally someone in the wedding must use crutches or a wheelchair. If your groom or either of your parents is in this situation, he or she should certainly play the traditional role in the service, with some modifications to make entering or leaving the site of the ceremony as easy as possible. With other friends and relatives, think of the individual cirumstances and the duties to be performed.

The feeling of being a part of the festivities and the aura of hope and happiness that only a bride and a groom will bring is a gift you will be giving your wedding party—and all your family and friends.

7
Guide to Wedding Clothes

Your dress sets the style of your wedding, and everyone else is outfitted accordingly. You may fall in love with a certain dress and plan your wedding around it. It could be regal satin, graced with a mantilla to the floor—so stately, it belongs at a very formal ceremony. Or it could be a wide-skirted cotton banded in pastel, suggesting a semiformal occasion outdoors. You might also, of course, decide the mood of the wedding, the time and place first, then shop for the prettiest and most appropriate look.

Styles of wedding dress change along with other fashions, but the pleasure of wearing a special and beautiful costume draws brides year after year to the traditional long dress and veil in one of the many lovely shadings of white.

Clothes for the groom and other men in the wedding party follow a traditional pattern as well. Yet with greater availability and a wider range of styles in men's wear today, you and your groom may also find a look somewhat different from the traditional formal wear. Colors, ruffles, and new fabrics are acceptable, so long as they complement the style of your dress.

Once, only the father of the bride dressed to match the other men in the wedding (because he escorts his daughter down the aisle, he is an official member of the wedding party). The father of the groom chose the kind of suit a guest might. Today, however, both fathers generally take their cues from the groomsmen, highlighting their honored roles and lending a uniform look to the occasion. In the event that contemporary suits are the choice, the fathers may want to wear traditional clothes, if this makes them feel more comfortable.

Bridesmaids have the greatest range of choice, but their dresses, too, should complement your own. This is why it is probably best that in shopping for maids' dresses, you and the honor attendant narrow the selection to about three you find appropriate, then let the bridesmaids make the final decision. Naturally the mothers of the bride and groom will want attire in harmony with the style of the wedding.

Proper dress varies with the hour and the season, but the wedding party will look most striking coming down the aisle and standing in the receiving line if they dress alike. Every usher is outfitted like the best man, each bridesmaid very much like the honor attendant, and both mothers appear in dresses of the same length and formality.

Very Formal Weddings

You'll look magnificent in a breathtaking dress of satin, lace, peau de soie, or another equally formal fabric. It will most likely be an elegant new design with a long, perhaps cathedral- or chapel-length, train; or in some cases, it may be an heirloom dress worn with pride by generations of brides. Very formal wedding dresses are almost always worn with a full-length veil and headpiece embellished with lace, beading, silk flowers, or even fur. You'll probably carry an elaborate bouquet of flowers or a flower-trimmed prayer book and wear simple shoes to match your dress. Gloves enhance the formality of a short-sleeved or sleeveless look. Jewelry is optional, but any you wear should be classic. You may move your engagement ring to your right hand until after the ceremony, when you'll return it to your left hand. Avoid wearing any ring on your right hand for the receiving line; it may prove painful when you shake hands with all your guests.

The groom and other men in the wedding party wear formal clothes, which they may rent. Everyone, including your father, dresses alike, but the neckwear and boutonnières may be varied slightly to distinguish the groom and best man from the other men. (His boutonnière might be stephanotis or another flower to match your bouquet; theirs, carnations, perhaps.) For ceremonies beginning before six o'clock in the evening, formal daytime wear consists of handsome black or oxford gray cutaway coat, gray and black striped trousers, gray waistcoat, and formal white shirt with a wing collar. Accessories include a striped silk ascot with a pearl or gold stickpin, gray gloves, black shoes, and black socks. Ushers sometimes wear starched, turned-down collars with striped four-in-hand ties in place of the wing collars and ascots worn by the groom and best man. Gray spats and black silk top hats are an optional part of this distinguished ensemble.

After six o'clock, correct dress for your groom and his attendants is the ultrasophisticated formal attire known as "white tie": a black tailcoat and matching satin-trimmed trousers, a white piqué waistcoat and a stiff-front shirt with a wing collar and French cuffs. Accessories include studs, a white piqué bow tie, white gloves, black patent leather pumps, and long black socks. A black silk top hat is optional for all but the most formal weddings.

Men who want a more contemporary look may wear colored, contoured long or short jackets, usually with wing-collared shirts.

The bridesmaids and your honor attendant wear elegant floor-length dresses in harmony with the feeling of your own dress. If you'll be in a classically rich silk, with an exquisitely rolled piping tracing empire lines, for example, think about linen—similarly unadorned—for your attendants. Or if you have decided on a look that is sculpted low in the bodice, theirs might drape low in the back. The maids usually wear identical dresses, but your honor attendant may be identified by a different shade, a contrasting color (deep rose instead of pink), or, for a more subtle distinction, the same dress as the maids'—with contrasting trim or accessories. Floral wreaths and ribbon headbands, lace hats and wisps of veiling, and three-cornered scarves all make attractive headpieces, as long as they match or harmonize with the dresses. The bridesmaids in a very formal wedding almost always wear gloves to complement short or sleeveless looks. Wrist-length white gloves are always correct and frequently the most attractive. Maids' shoes should be simple and match the mood and color of their dresses. Attendants' jewelry is always uniform (a gift from the bride, perhaps) and usually light and delicate looking.

Junior bridesmaids may wear adaptations of the bridesmaids' outfits, styled along more youthful lines. Their dresses should be of the same color and, if possible, the same fabric as those of your other attendants. Their flowers and headpieces may match as well. Flat-heeled shoes tend to be more suitable than high heels.

Flower girls and young girls serving as pages or in other important roles often wear floor-length dresses patterned after the bridesmaids' dresses. But almost any party dress is suitable. A flower girl's outfit may be the same color as the maids', or she may wear a frilly white dress trimmed and sashed in a matching shade. As long as she does not scatter any petals (it isn't safe), she may carry them in the traditional basket. But a dainty old-fashioned nosegay or flower muff may be easier for her to handle. She also wears a floral or ribbon headband, white gloves, and white or pastel party shoes.

Ring bearers (or boy pages) will be charming in the satin and velvet suits once traditional. Or, if the little boys don't feel comfortable in unfamiliar clothes, they might wear dark blue Eton suits, white shorts, and white or blue knee socks. For a summer wedding, a young boy might appear in a white linen suit with white knee socks and white shoes. If the style of the men is contemporary wedding dress, young boys may be outfitted in matching formal suits, especially if they're likely to be better behaved sporting long pants and jacket "just like Dad's."

The mothers of the bride and groom always wear pretty, floor-length dinner or evening dresses to a very formal wedding. The styles may be less formal for a daytime wedding than for an evening ceremony, but the length remains the same. Almost any flattering color, except all-black or all-white, is appropriate, but rather than match the wedding party (or each other), the color should be one that blends with that of the bride's attendants. The mothers may wear small hats or veils, simple shoes and gloves, and carry or wear flowers, as long as their looks are similarly accessorized. Incidentally, the mother of the bride selects her outfit first, then describes it to the mother of the groom, so she can choose hers. It is important that the mother of the bride give the mother of the groom ample time to shop.

If they take part in the ceremony, as in the Jewish service, the mothers entrust their handbags and wraps to a seated family member.

Formal Weddings

You'll look every inch a bride in a traditional, floor-length wedding dress, most likely with a chapel-length or sweep train. A formal wedding dress is a little less elaborate than that worn in a very formal wedding and will probably be accompanied by a veil or mantilla to the hem, but shorter veils—shoulder-length or fingertip-length, for instance—and hats are also lovely. If the sleeves of your dress are less than full-length, you may wear gloves in white kid, lace, or fabric to match your dress. Your bouquet may be simpler than one you'd carry at a very formal wedding, but your shoes and all other accessories are the same.

Undergarments for the wedding dress should be chosen with a critical eye—a sheer, blousy bodice may call for a pretty camisole; a clinging fabric may need special attention to stockings and slip to preserve the formality of the look down to the last detail.

The groom, fathers, and other men in your wedding party dress according to the season and the hour of the ceremony. For a formal daytime wedding, the traditional attire includes a black or oxford gray sack coat or stroller (styled like a regular suit jacket and just as comfortable), striped trousers, gray waistcoat, and white shirt with a turned-down collar and French cuffs, plus a striped four-in-hand tie, gray gloves, black shoes, and black socks. The accompanying Homburg hat may be omitted.

For a formal ceremony beginning after six o'clock, the men wear "black tie": a black dinner jacket with matching trousers, white pleated-front shirt with a turned-down collar and French cuffs, and a black vest or cummerbund. Black shoes, socks, and bow tie are the traditional accessories, along with chamois or gray gloves. For a summer wedding, your groom and his men could opt for white dinner jackets, wear a cummerbund in place of a vest, and leave off the gloves.

When the men wish a more contemporary look, this usually means it will be a formal wedding. They may wear colored formal suits, dress shirts, bow ties, and vests or cummerbunds. And to indicate his role, the groom may want to wear a different—but harmonizing—suit or jacket altogether.

Confused about which formal suit is right if the ceremony will begin before six, the reception after? Always select the look according to the time of the ceremony.

The bridesmaids and honor attendants dress much the same as for a very formal wedding, in floor-length dresses, complementary headpieces and shoes. Gloves are optional for a formal wedding, and the style of dress is usually a little less ornate than for a very formal ceremony. They may, for example, carry parasols with summery styles. If your wedding is very small or early in the day, street-length or cocktail-length dresses are a possibility.

In shopping, you may find that bridesmaids' dresses are made to match your own. This can be an enormous help in creating a unified look for the wedding party. A formal wedding does, however, allow you to choose a slightly less elaborate mood for them if it means they will then be able to wear their dresses again.

The mothers of the bride and groom usually wear long dinner dresses to a formal evening wedding, and street-length or cocktail-length outfits for daytime ceremonies. Either is correct as long as both mothers dress similarly. It is courteous to keep in mind that the mothers set the style for the guests—the mothers may choose to appear in the kinds of outfits they know their guests will feel comfortable in for the occasion. The mothers, again, dress in complementary but not matching colors: one in beige, perhaps, the other in peach; or one in aqua, the other in emerald.

Small hats or veils were once customary at a church ceremony, but are now often optional. They are unnecessary when the wedding takes place at another location. Guidelines for other accessories are the same as those for mothers at a very formal wedding.

Semiformal Weddings

You may wear an elaborate short dress or a simple floor-length dress with a train. Picture a wispy chiffon, a sleek pour of jersey, lace crochet from neckline to hem. Your accessories, including your flowers, are simpler than those for a formal wedding. With a street-length dress, a short veil is best; with a long dress, you may choose a veil reaching farther. Hats or flowers for the hair are also lovely.

The groom and his attendants traditionally wear solid dark suits in the day, with plain white shirts, four-in-hand ties, and black shoes with long socks. It is not necessary for their ties to match, but an overall effect should be achieved—rather than a mix of bright paisley or colorful stripes, somewhat similar club ties, perhaps. For a summer wedding, the men may look cool and crisp in white linen jackets with oxford gray trousers or dark blue jackets with gray or white flannel trousers. They may prefer dinner jackets or contemporary formal suits with dress shirts, bow ties, vests or cummerbunds, especially in the evening. It is an evening wedding? Then black tie appropriate to the season is also a good-looking possibility.

The honor attendant and bridesmaids, if any, wear street-length or very simple, long dresses in harmony with that of the bride. Shoes and jewelry should complement their dresses. Gloves and hats or flowers for the hair are optional. Attendants at a semiformal wedding may carry small bouquets or wear flowers at their collars, waists, or wrists.

Children seldom participate in either semiformal or informal weddings unless they are children of the bride and groom. In this case, they dress as they would for any special occasion.

The mothers wear street-length or long dresses similar to that of the honor attendant.

Informal Weddings

You may choose a becoming street-length outfit appropriate to the season. A suit or jacketed dress is the most polished look. It may be in white or any color except black. Accessories include flowers to wear instead of to carry.

The groom and his best man usually wear their best dark suits.

The honor attendant dresses in a style similar to that of the bride.

The mothers wear street-length outfits similar to that of the honor attendant.

Having something very special—and probably new—helps make a wedding the celebration it is. In addition to choosing clothes with care, the people involved should allow a day or two off in the final week of planning to rest and relax. That way the bride and everyone from mothers to maids will be assured of hearing the time-honored compliment, "You look beautiful!"

8
Your Wedding Ceremony

This is the big moment, one of the richest experiences the two of you will ever share. To ensure you'll have the beautiful ceremony you want, make an appointment to speak to your minister, priest, rabbi, or judge as soon as possible. Discuss the significance of the vows you'll recite; what, if any, individual changes or additions you'd like (a meaningful prayer or poem, a musical interlude, perhaps the exchange of vows you've written yourselves); and what each of you would like your ceremony to express about yourselves, your families, and the marriage you plan.

Your Rehearsal

Here is your chance to practice for the "real thing," an opportunity for you and your groom and all the members of the wedding, including musicians, ushers, and clergy, to smooth out all the last-minute details.

The marriage service will not be read in full at the rehearsal, but you'll go over any special variations you've requested, to pick up the cues for your responses, and to outline the roles of the honor attendant and the best man. This is the time to make certain anyone who must do something unique—light a candle to symbolize the joining of families, start the "kiss of peace" among guests—does a run-through of his or her part.

The clergy (or wedding consultant, if you have one) can brief the ushers on the procedure for seating guests and give instructions to those with special duties like spreading the aisle canvas or pew ribbons. It helps, of course, if the best man has familiarized himself with these details ahead of time. "Where can people get a drink of water?" and "When do we start letting everybody out?" are the kinds of questions that are likely to come up.

Incidentally, it may be a good idea to take along dummy bouquets—perhaps made from gift-ribbon bows. This way you and your attendants can practice passing your flowers as well as trying the turns necessary at the altar. As one whose actions will be interpreted as signals to guests, your mother will want to know at what points the clergy will say such things as, "All rise."

Afterward, you will probably all celebrate with a rehearsal dinner. Many couples believe that the rehearsal and dinner must be the night before the ceremony. If possible, schedule your rehearsal two nights before the ceremony so the party can continue as long as everyone wishes, without worry about having to hurry home to get a good night's rest. Not possible? At least make certain you and your groom leave on time.

Seating for the Ceremony

In a Christian wedding, the left side of the church is reserved for the bride's family and friends, the right side for the groom's. In Conservative and Orthodox Jewish weddings, it is the reverse.

(If one family will be having many more guests than the other, of course, everyone may sit together.) Your parents sit in the first pews on their respective sides, grandparents in the second pews to ensure they'll get the best view—along the aisle. You may wish to reserve additional pews on each side for other close relatives and friends.

The section reserved for family is often marked with flowers or ribbons, and pew cards or "within the ribbons" cards may be sent to those guests you wish to honor with these special seats. All other guests are seated from front to back as they enter the church. Late-arriving guests should slip into the back rows, as no one should be seated after the bride's mother.

Ceremony Timetable

Study this sample countdown based on a large formal wedding taking place about fifteen minutes from the bride's house. Adapt it to your own situation, allowing plenty of time—even if traffic is heavy—to arrive at the church relaxed and ready.

Two hours before the ceremony: You, your mother, and your attendants begin dressing. If you're getting ready at the ceremony site, plan to arrive there at least an hour and a half before the ceremony.

One hour before the ceremony: Any bridesmaids who've dressed elsewhere gather at your house to pick up their flowers and pose for pictures.

Forty-five minutes before the ceremony: The ushers arrive at the ceremony site and pin on their boutonnières. They distribute Mass books and wedding programs, pick up seating plans from the head usher, then gather near the entrance to wait for guests to arrive.

Thirty minutes before the ceremony: The organist starts to play the prelude while the ushers escort guests to their seats. Your mother and attendants leave for the church.

Twenty minutes before the ceremony: The groom and his best man arrive. The clergy checks the marriage license (if he or she has not already done so), receives the fee from the best man, and issues any last-minute instructions. Meanwhile, you and your father leave for the church.

Ten minutes before the ceremony: Your attendants arrive at the church, followed by your mother, the groom's parents, and other close members of your families. The bridal party and the parents wait in the vestibule while the other relatives are seated.

Five minutes before the ceremony: The groom's mother is escorted to her seat. The groom's father follows a few feet behind the usher, then takes his seat beside his wife. You and your father arrive and, if possible, park at a back entrance where you won't be seen by late-arriving guests (you want to surprise everyone!). As your mother—the last person seated by an usher—starts down the aisle, you and your father join the wedding party in the vestibule.

One minute before the ceremony: Two ushers walk in step to the front of the aisle to lay the aisle ribbons and canvas, if either is used. They then return to the vestibule and take their places in the procession.

Ceremony time: The minister, priest, or rabbi takes his place, followed by the groom and the best man. The procession begins, and all turn to watch.

In some areas and within some families, the groom's parents will be in front of the church to greet the guests. And especially if the ceremony is held at a site other than a church, the couple as well as both sets of parents may mingle with guests before the actual start of the service. People in this situation are urged to draw up a suitable timetable of preceremony details.

Transportation

A note about the cars. A fleet of chauffeur-driven limousines— probably rented—are part of what can make a wedding ultra-elegant. There is one for the bride and her father, one for the mother of the bride and the bride's attendants, one for the groom's parents, and one or two for the groom and his attendants. The limousines appear at their various pick-up points ten minutes before departure time. When a single chauffeured car is hired, it carries the bride and her father to the church, waits outside until the bride and groom dash out from the ceremony, then takes them on to the reception. Friends who are not members of the wedding party can also provide transportation using their own cars; being relieved of the responsibility of maneuvering through heavy traffic means the mother of the groom, for instance, will arrive feeling relaxed and fresh. Drivers should be given money for a car wash and a full tank of gas, complete instructions with addresses and phone numbers of all the people they are to pick up, and perhaps a special gift of thanks.

The Procession

In the Protestant service, the ushers enter from the back of the church first, in pairs, with the shortest of them leading. The bridesmaids follow individually, when there are fewer than four; otherwise, they are often paired much like the ushers. Instead of the old-fashioned "hesitation step," they may walk slowly and naturally along with the music. If there is an odd usher or maid, the shortest attendant leads off alone. The honor attendant comes next, then the ring bearer, then the flower girls. Now the bride and her father enter, with the pages, if any, carrying the bride's train behind her. As you wait for this moment, remember it is a sensitive—and proud—time for your father; a loving squeeze of his hand may mean a lot to him.

Catholic brides and grooms frequently observe the same procedure, but they may forego the traditional procession and be met at the church door by the priest.

All Jewish processions, Orthodox, Conservative, and Reform, vary according to local custom and to the preferences of the family. In the simplest service, the ushers lead the procession in pairs,

CHRISTIAN PROCESSION:
1) Bride, 2) Father of the Bride,
3) Flower Girl, 4) Ring Bearer,
5) Honor Attendant, 6)
Bridesmaids, 7) Ushers, 8)
Groom, 9) Best Man, 10)
Wedding Official.

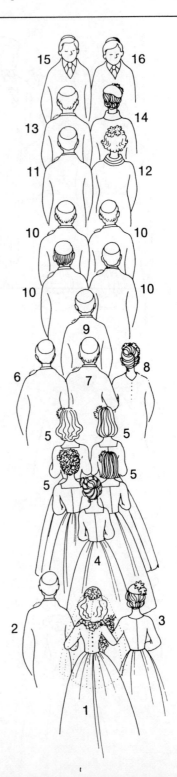

TRADITIONAL JEWISH PROCESSION: 1) Bride, 2) Father of the Bride, 3) Mother of the Bride, 4) Honor Attendant, 5) Bridesmaids, 6) Groom, 7) Father of the Groom, 8) Mother of the Groom, 9) Best Man, 10) Ushers, 11) Groom's Grandfather, 12) Groom's Grandmother, 13) Bride's Grandfather, 14) Bride's Grandmother, 15) Cantor, 16) Rabbi. (Note: If a Flower Girl and Ring Bearer participate, they immediately precede the bride and her parents.)

followed by the bridesmaids in pairs. Then come the groom and his best man, the honor attendant, the flower girl, and the bride on her father's right. The groom's parents and the bride's mother may join in the procession and stand under the *huppah,* or canopy, during the ceremony.

The most elaborate Jewish ceremony is led by the rabbi and cantor, followed by the couple's grandparents, the ushers, the bridesmaids, the best man, the groom and his parents, the bride's honor attendant, her flower girl, and the bride with her parents. Your rabbi will tell you how he prefers to organize the procession, taking into account the local customs and the amount of space available for the wedding party.

Civil ceremonies are usually quite small, with the bride preceded by one attendant and escorted into the room by her father. For a large civil ceremony in a ballroom or other formal setting, choose the procession format that seems suitable to your needs and to the ceremony setting.

Altar Procedures

When the bridal party reaches the first row of seats, they traditionally form one of two arrangements: the ushers turn to the right to create a diagonal line behind the groom and best man, while the bridesmaids assemble in a similar line on the left side; or each pair of attendants separates at the altar, with one pair going to each side. Ushers and maids may stand side by side, or the bridesmaids may stand one step in front of the ushers. Another contemporary variation is for the bridesmaids and ushers to gather in a semicircle around the bride and groom, facing the congregation. Children may stand at the altar through the ceremony, but they're frequently happier if allowed to slide into the second or third pew with their parents.

In the Protestant service, you leave your father's arm and take one step forward as you reach the head of the aisle. The groom comes forward to join you on your right. The honor attendant and best man take their positions on either side of the bride and groom, while the other attendants turn toward the altar. Your father remains standing one step behind and to your left until the minister asks, "Who gives this woman to be married?" He replies, "I do," or "Her mother and I do," then takes his seat next to your mother in the first pew. As a contemporary alternative to the giving-away, the minister might ask, "Who blesses this marriage?" Both your and your groom's parents reply, "We, their parents, do."

In Catholic ceremonies, where the bride is not actually given away, your father turns and joins your mother as soon as you have reached the altar. In the Jewish ceremony, all the parents remain standing throughout.

CHRISTIAN CEREMONY AT THE ALTAR: 1) Bride, 2) Father of the Bride, 3) Flower Girl, 4) Ring Bearer, 5) Honor Attendant, 6) Bridesmaids, 7) Ushers, 8) Groom, 9) Best Man, 10) Wedding Official. (Note: Father of the Bride takes his seat following the giving-away.)

JEWISH WEDDING: 1) Bride, 2) Father of the Bride, 3) Mother of the Bride, 4) Honor Attendant, 5) Bridesmaids, 6) Groom, 7) Father of the Groom, 8) Mother of the Groom, 9) Best Man, 10) Ushers, 11) Rabbi. (Note: Grandparents of the bride and groom may take their seats after the procession; the Cantor takes his appropriate place.)

If you are required to kneel or climb steps during the ceremony, your groom will take your arm to help you up and down. Then, when the ceremony is over and the official has congratulated the two of you, your groom or honor attendant lifts your face veil, if you are wearing one, for the traditional kiss. (It is not mandatory that you kiss, but it is a long-loved tradition that says it's time to celebrate!) The honor attendant puts your bouquet in your right hand and arranges your train as you turn to face your guests for the recessional—with a smile.

The Recessional

When the organist sounds the happy signal, you take your groom's right arm and start up the aisle together. Your attendants, starting with the children if they have remained at the altar, quickly fall into step behind you: the honor attendant on the right arm of the best man, each bridesmaid on the arm of an usher, and extra ushers walking together at the end.

On reaching the vestibule, the ushers you've designated in advance return to escort the mothers and honored guests from the church and to roll up any pew ribbons. You, your groom, and your honor attendants will probably join the clergy in his or her chambers to sign the marriage license. You and the wedding party may wish to return to the church to pose for photographs, as well. In the meantime, guests may wait in front of the church for you to appear to receive their hugs and clapping and laughter, or the ushers delegated to do so direct guests to the reception site.

If the marriage license has been signed prior to the ceremony (perhaps at the rehearsal dinner), you may form a receiving line immediately after the ceremony, in the vestibule or in front of the church. Or you and the bridesmaids may dash immediately into your waiting cars—and off to the reception! There, you'll have time to pose for pictures, freshen your makeup, and form the receiving line before guests arrive. The ushers stay at the church to see that it is cleared of guests and any of their belongings before they head on to the reception.

Special Variations

If your parents are divorced, your father may still escort you down the aisle and give you away. He then sits down in the third pew, with his wife if he has remarried. Your mother sits in the first pew. The choice of escort is yours, however, and if you prefer, your stepfather or another male relative may walk you down the aisle. In the Jewish procession, the parent and stepparent who raised you take part and all grandparents may be seated in equally honored positions. The divorced parents are still friendly? Of course, they may sit together. The most important thing is that everyone—including the bride—feels comfortable and happy. Similar guidelines apply if the groom's parents are divorced.

If your father has died, you may ask your stepfather, brother, uncle, or other close relative, a family friend, or an usher to escort you. Your mother may also walk you to the altar if she feels comfortable with this idea. Your stepfather, should you feel close to him, or your mother, may give you away as well. Ask your mother if she would prefer to simply nod or say "I do" from her seat in the first pew, or if she would like the best man to escort her to your side at the appropriate moment in the ceremony.

If the church has two center aisles, you may use the left aisle

RECESSIONAL: 1) Bride, 2) Groom, 3) Flower Girl, 4) Ring Bearer, 5) Honor Attendant, 6) Best Man, 7) Bridesmaids, 8) Ushers.

for the procession and the right aisle for the recessional, or close off the second aisle entirely. When both aisles are used, the bride's relatives and friends sit on both sides of the left aisle, the groom's on both sides of the right aisle. The parents sit in the center section; the bride's on the left, the groom's on the right.

If you are personalizing your ceremony, you may walk in alone, on your groom's arm, or with both parents, as is the Jewish tradition.

Semiformal Weddings

Most formal wedding procedures also apply to the smaller, semiformal wedding. With fewer guests, you may omit the pew ribbons and aisle carpet, especially since you probably will not be wearing a dress with a train. (For details on semiformal home garden weddings, see Chapter 10.)

Informal Weddings

An intimate, informal wedding may be held at home, in a small chapel, a judge's chambers, or your favorite restaurant or club. Guests may be welcomed and directed to the wedding area by your mother, your honor attendant, or by another close friend or relative. You and your groom may enjoy mingling before the ceremony or you may wait in another room, where your best friends may come to help you make sure your eye makeup is the way you want and that you haven't forgotten "something borrowed." At ceremony time, the two of you, your honor attendant, and the best man take your places before the ceremony official. Your groom or your father may escort you, if you wish. After the ceremony and the traditional kiss, you simply turn to greet your guests and receive their heartfelt good wishes.

Informal or formal, your ceremony will no doubt remind all your guests of their own marriage vows or their sentiments regarding family and friendships. In this way, your wedding can be rich with meaning for everyone.

9
Religious Rituals

While American marriage ceremonies share many similarities, there are differences among religions. And even within the same faith, local customs may influence the style of the wedding. It is important, therefore, to discuss the details of your ceremony with the proper church officials as soon as possible. If you and your fiancé are regular members of the church, you'll want to explore the relationship of the service—and the church itself—to the family you are now forming. If you are not members, you may wish to make certain that the practices of the church in which you hope to marry reflect your personal beliefs. Here is a brief guide to the wedding ceremonies of major American religions today.

Protestant Weddings

Almost all Protestant churches use the standard ("Dearly Beloved. . .") wedding service, and most require the congregation to stand during part of the ceremony. Although there are no laws which prohibit marriage on particular days of the year, many of the Protestant clergy are reluctant to perform wedding ceremonies on Sundays and other religious holidays. Rules on music vary, but prior approval of a church authority may be required for the use of secular music, especially any modern, popular songs you may have in mind. There are no specific rules on attire, but bare-backed or strapless dresses may need a little jacket or wrap until reception time. (Many dresses for brides, bridesmaids, and mothers come with cover-ups for this very reason.) The following variations can be found among some of the Protestant faiths.

Episcopal: The Episcopal church usually discourages formal weddings during Lent. Often, too, at least one party to the marriage must have been baptized, and a number of premarital meetings with the priest may be required. The remarriage of divorced persons is customarily allowed, but dispensations are sometimes needed. A Nuptial Mass similar to the Catholic ceremony may be part of a wedding in the "High" or Anglo-Catholic branch of the Episcopal church.

Quaker: A Quaker wedding requires prior approval (which may take up to three months) from the monthly meeting of the Society of Friends. The marriage itself usually takes place during a meeting of worship where those in attendance meditate quietly. The bridal couple may enter the meeting together and join the circle of Friends already seated. The usual procession is another option; in this case, the bridal party then take seats on benches facing the meeting. After the traditional Quaker silence, the bride and groom rise, join hands, and say their vows. The groom speaks his promises first, then the bride. The bride is not given away nor does a third person pronounce them married, for the Friends believe that only God can create such a union.

Further details of the Quaker wedding are usually worked out in advance between the couple and an appointed group of meeting members. In a typical wedding, the marriage certificate is brought to the couple to sign after they have shared their vows. The certificate is then read aloud by a member of the meeting. The meeting may continue until the bride and groom feel ready to leave. All guests sign the marriage certificate before departing, which is a custom couples marrying in the Quaker faith may particularly treasure.

Neither a bridal party nor the exchange of rings is necessary at a Quaker wedding, but both are frequently seen today. When the meeting has a pastor, he naturally takes part in the ceremony and in the pre-wedding discussions. The use of music and floral decorations is left up to the couple to decide, but the wedding is a simple one—very much in the Quaker tradition.

Christian Scientist: Readers of the Christian Science faith are not ordained and may not perform marriages. When members of the faith marry, the ceremony may be performed by any minister ordained in another denomination or by proper legal authority. Readers and members of the Christian Scientist congregation can be a helpful source of those willing to officiate and to create an especially meaningful service for the bride and groom.

Mormon: The Church of Jesus Christ of Latter Day Saints recognizes two kinds of marriage. The first is for the faithful deemed fit for marriage by members of the Holy Priesthood; this wedding takes place in the temples of the church. Such couples are wed "for time and eternity" (instead of "until death you do part"). Their children are believed to belong to them for all eternity as well. The second is a civil ceremony performed by bishops of the church or other legal authorities. These couples are sometimes rewed in the temple at a later date. A Mormon and a non-Mormon may be wed in such a civil ceremony.

Roman Catholic Weddings

When both the bride and the groom are Catholic, the banns (intentions to marry) are published in the parish churches of both. These announcements may be made from the pulpit at the principal Masses on three consecutive Sundays or Holy Days before the wedding, or published in the church calendar or bulletin. The banns are not usually proclaimed for a mixed marriage. The non-Catholic party to a mixed marriage need not be baptized, but must be free to marry in a Catholic church, which means the Catholic party will first have to obtain a dispensation by the bishop of the diocese. It is easily secured these days, and the priest who will marry you will most likely handle the procedure. Couples who will marry in the Catholic church generally are required to attend a series of pre-wedding sessions before they receive permission for the wedding. The couple may be asked to bring as many practical issues—money management, for example—to the surface as spiritual issues, and they may find this kind of communication invaluable to their relationship. The marriage of divorced persons is usually not allowed in the church unless the previous marriage has been declared null before a Church court.

A Catholic bride must have the permission of her own pastor to be married in another parish. The officiating priest will need proof of baptism for baptized persons and evidence of freedom to marry. Catholic weddings are rarely conducted outside the church, although mixed marriages are sometimes performed in the church of the non-Catholic. In such cases, a Roman Catholic priest may officiate with the non-Catholic minister, pronouncing a prayer or blessing over the couple.

The procession for a Catholic wedding may follow the procedures for a Protestant ceremony, except that the bride is not given away. Some couples choose to be greeted at the vestibule door by the priest, then led by him to the altar. Many of the traditional wedding marches are not allowed in some Catholic dioceses since, as opera themes, they are secular rather than religious. (See Chapter 13 for alternatives and consult the officiating priest.)

While Catholic marriages may be performed and Nuptial Masses celebrated during Lent and Advent, the decoration of the church and the style of the wedding may be somewhat restricted. A profusion of gaily colored flowers, for instance, may be discouraged in favor of the more subtle beauty of white ones.

A Nuptial Mass may be arranged for almost any Catholic wedding, with the brief wedding ceremony being incorporated into the Mass. Non-Catholics at a Nuptial Mass (including the bride or groom if it is a mixed marriage) do not take Communion. Mass books, which may be imprinted with the names of the bridal couple and the date of the ceremony, are often distributed to guests so they may follow the ritual of the Mass. Non-Catholic guests needn't give the responses, but they may kneel (or sit quietly while others kneel) and stand at the proper times in the ceremony.

Incidentally, altar boys should be given a tip or appropriate gift —the best man can pass it along.

Eastern Orthodox Weddings

The churches of the Eastern Rite, including Greek and Russian Orthodox, are similar in some ways to the Catholic Church. Mixed marriages are allowed, but the non-Orthodox party to the marriage must be a baptized Christian. Eastern Rite churches permit the remarriage of those who've received religious decrees of annulment following a civil divorce. The banns of marriage may be proclaimed, but are not necessary.

Orthodox weddings usually take place in the afternoon or early evening and may not be solemnized in church during any season of fasting, on the eve of certain holy days, during the week after Easter, or in the two weeks after Christmas. They seldom include the liturgy, as the marriage itself is a long ceremony rich with symbolism and pageantry. Traditionally, the only music allowed in an Orthodox church is that of an unaccompanied choir and the singing of the ancient Byzantine and Russian chants. However, organs are now used in some American Greek churches.

The standard wedding procession in which the bride's father gives her away is customary in the Greek ceremony. In the Russian ceremony, the wedding party is met at the vestibule door by the priest, and the bride is given away before the procession proceeds. The size of the wedding party and its arrangement are matters of personal taste and local custom, with the honor attendant and best man frequently having somewhat more complex duties during the ceremony. Traditionally, a Greek bride wears a face veil, but a Russian bride need not. The guests at a Russian Orthodox wedding usually remain standing during the ceremony, but in Greek churches in America, they are often allowed to sit during the less sacred parts of the service.

An Orthodox wedding begins with a betrothal ritual, usually at the front or center of the church. This includes the blessing and exchange of the rings, which are customarily worn by both bride and groom on their right hands. The rings are exchanged between bride and groom three times to signify the Holy Trinity.

At the close of the betrothal ritual, the bride and groom move up the center aisle of the church to positions before the altar screen or *ikonostasis*. Two crowns are placed on the heads of the bride and groom and exchanged three times in the Greek ceremony. In the Russian ceremony, the honor attendant and the best man hold the crowns above the couple's heads. After the Gospel is read, a cup of wine is shared three times by the bride and groom to symbolize the joys and the sorrows they will share in marriage. Afterward, in the Greek ceremony, the wine is also drunk by the best man. The bride and groom are then led around a ceremonial table three times with their hands bound. At the close of the ceremony, the congregation joins in singing "God Grant Them Many Years."

After the recessional in a Greek church, friends of the family often stand on the church steps and distribute festive packets of candy to the other guests. This has the same significance as the shower of rice tradition originated among the Chinese: "May you always enjoy a life of plenty."

Jewish Weddings

No single set of rules applies to all Jewish weddings, for there are differences among the Orthodox, Conservative, and Reform branches of the faith. Individual rabbis and synagogues also have their own interpretations, so verification of all guidelines and procedures with the officiating rabbi before plans are finalized is wise. Rabbis, as a rule, will not perform mixed marriages, and Orthodox and Conservative rabbis do not recognize any divorces except those granted by religious decree. Reform clergy, however, often recognize civil divorces.

Jewish weddings may take place at any time except on the Sabbath (from sundown on Friday to sundown on Saturday), on Holy Days, during a three-week period in midsummer, and during almost all of Passover and Shabuoth. Most weddings are celebrated on Saturday evening after sundown or on Sunday. A Jewish wedding may occur almost anywhere, so many are not performed in synagogues or temples. It is more usual in some localities for the ceremony to take place at a club, hotel, or catering hall where the centuries-old splendor of the wedding feast and dancing may follow. Conventional wedding attire, including a face veil for the bride if she is Orthodox, is generally worn. In Conservative and Orthodox ceremonies both, all the men—including those in the wedding party—cover their heads with either *yarmulkes* or silk top hats.

In Jewish tradition, the bride and groom may not see each other before the ceremony, yet the bride and her attendants may wait, in all their finery, in a separate room where they sometimes receive guests beforehand. At the appropriate time, the bride's family will be seated on the right side of the hall or temple, the groom's family on the left, before any other guests are shown to their places.

The order of the procession and positions during the ceremony are set by local custom, with Orthodox and Conservative processions usually including the groom and both sets of parents (see Chapter 8). The ushers walk down the aisle first, followed by the bridesmaids, then the ring bearer. Sometimes the ushers and maids form a guard of honor through which the rest of the wedding party will pass.

Jewish marriages are traditionally performed under a *huppah*, a heavily ornamented canopy symbolizing shelter from the open sky in nomadic times, and today, the home the couple will live in together. The *huppah* may also be embellished with—or woven entirely of—fresh flowers. It is usually placed in front of an attractive background at one end of the room or in front of the Ark in a temple. The procession walks toward the canopy, with each person taking a prescribed position under or near it.

The bride stands on the groom's right under the canopy, and the rabbi faces them. It is also customary for the honor attendants to be under the *huppah*—the bride's attendant on her right, the groom's best man on his left. When space permits, the parents sometimes gather alongside or directly behind their children under the *huppah*. The bridesmaids and ushers usually line up in single file on either side of the canopy, as shown in the illustration in Chapter 8).

During the wedding ceremony, the rabbi stands next to a small table covered in white and set with cups of ritual wine and a glass, frequently wrapped in a piece of white silk or a napkin. The service begins with a betrothal ceremony, then an introductory blessing. Next, the groom sips from the glass of wine and passes it to the bride. After the couple have said their vows, the groom places a plain gold band on the bride's right index finger in the Conservative and Orthodox ceremony, on her left hand in the Reform ceremony. Conservative and Orthodox rabbis now read the *ketubah*, or traditional marriage contract. How much of the service is conducted in English, how much in Hebrew may vary. But all Jewish ceremonies end with the traditional Seven Blessings, the last of which includes the ritual crushing of the wine glass beneath the groom's heel, an address by the rabbi to the couple, and closing benediction. At that, *"mazel tov"* will sound from all corners of the room, as guests call out their best wishes to the bride and groom.

The order of the recessional may differ, but it is always led by the bride and groom. They are usually followed by the bride's parents, the groom's parents, the maid or matron of honor on the best man's arm, then the rabbi, with pairs of bridesmaids and ushers bringing up the rear.

In a Reform wedding, the procession, recessional, and other ceremony details are frequently quite close to those used in the Protestant service, including the use of the traditional wedding marches. There may be a double ring ceremony, and the marriage may or may not be performed under a *huppah*.

The wedding feast is traditionally very important to a Jewish wedding. Frequently most lavish, it always includes a marriage grace or blessing at some point in the dining. The receiving line and other details are similar to those for any kind of reception.

The Interfaith Wedding

When the bride and groom are of different faiths, it is possible for them to be married in a ceremony which combines the two. The interfaith wedding, sometimes known as the ecumenical service among Christian groups, can take several forms depending on your own wishes and those of the clergy involved. The ceremony can be performed almost entirely by the official of one faith, with the other one giving a short blessing at the end. For example, the couple might be married by a Catholic priest according to the ritual of the Mass, and have a rabbi present to offer the Hebrew Seven Blessings after the vows are exchanged. Or, the service can be divided equally between the two faiths, with a minister and priest, perhaps, alternating religious readings and then joining together for the exchange of vows and the ring ceremony.

It is doubly important when considering an interfaith ceremony to begin your plans early. First, check to make sure that your own clergy agree to participate. More and more clergy are willing to take part in this type of service, but there are individuals who prefer not to. Also keep in mind, for both religions, the days of the calendar when marriages may not be permitted. In planning the actual ceremony, work closely with the clergy to be sure that the final service is one that is both acceptable and meaningful to everyone present.

The Religious Wedding Personalized

Almost all religions allow certain variations in their ceremonies; many even have several services from which you might choose. You and your fiancé should discuss the standard vows. Is this what you want your wedding to express? If you wish changes —and they can be accomplished with dignity—alterations in the wedding service can greatly enrich this day in your memory. (Some of the classic additions to the wedding service are mentioned briefly in Chapter 8.) A special rose given to each mother after the giving-away, a hymn sung by guests—these are the kinds of ideas the clergy may also be able to suggest. In trying to involve your guests, do consider the sensitivities of your own family and friends. Asking them to renew their vows aloud may sound like a wonderful thing, but they may not feel comfortable doing so. They may also be somewhat embarrassed if your vows become very personal or go on at length (an hour for your total ceremony is probably the upper limit).

The wedding ceremony may seem brief, but the ritual, the symbolism, the tradition create a connection that has lasted for centuries among all those who have married and will continue on in the future. It is this realization that can touch everyone at your ceremony in a quiet and marvelous way.

10
Special Weddings

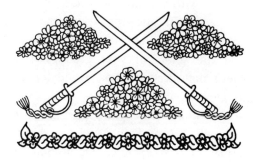

Marry in the warm and comfortable setting of home, amidst the splendor of a military service, or outdoors under an open sky. You may choose the special setting and touches of individuality that will make your wedding most significant to you and your fiancé. There are several classic variations to the traditional ceremony you may want to think about.

The Military Wedding

The flourish of a military wedding with its famous arch of sabers (swords in the Navy) appeals to many brides who marry commissioned officers on active duty. The arch, under which the bride and groom walk at the end of the ceremony, is formed by the fellow officers of the groom, who also serve as ushers.

A groom in any branch of military service, whether an officer or not, may be married in uniform, but swords and sabers are carried only by officers in full dress uniform (blue in winter, white in summer). Do you wish to have your brothers or other close friends who are not officers in the military participate? They wear traditional formal attire. As a rule, however, your father is the only man in the procession in civilian clothes. Instead of boutonnières, military decorations are worn by men in uniform.

Since full dress military uniforms are very formal, you might complement the men with the utmost in elegance—a long dress of satin, velvet, or lace with flowing train and veil. Dress your bridesmaids and honor attendant in equally formal long dresses, perhaps matching the colors of your groom's academy. Mothers and wedding guests may dress as they would for any other formal wedding at the same hour and season.

Many military weddings take place at military chapels, including those at Annapolis, West Point, and the Air Force Academy, but other locations are acceptable. Decorations usually include the American flag and the standards of the groom's unit, in addition to flowers. Do verify all your plans, of course, with the proper military authorities.

Invitations and announcements differ only in that the groom's rank and service are indicated. If your fiancé is a junior officer (below the rank of Army or Air Force Captain or Naval Commander), his title appears under his name, followed by the branch of service on the same line. "Mr." is never used to address or refer to an officer on active duty. (See Chapter 5 for further details on the use of military titles.)

The military procession follows standard procedures, but the recessional is dramatized by the traditional arch of steel. And with the regalia of the men's clothes and the flash of metal in the sun, this is truly a memorable sight for guests. The arch may be formed outside the church, in front of the chancel—or both—depending on church rules, the branch of service, and personal preference. The head usher usually issues the commands, starting with "Center face," the signal to form two facing lines. When the order "Arch sabers" (or "Draw swords") is given, each usher raises his saber in his right hand, cutting edge on top. After you and your groom have passed under the arch, sabers are sheathed and returned to the "carry" position. If the arch will be formed outside as well, the bride and groom wait in the vestibule until the ushers are in place at the chapel door or on the steps.

At the reception following a military wedding, you might feature regimental decorations and music, including miniature flags and the theme song of the groom's branch of the service. At a seated reception, military guests are shown to their places in order of rank. The highlight of the reception comes when the bride and groom cut the cake using the groom's saber or sword.

Should the bride and her attendants be officers in the military, they usually choose to wear traditional wedding dress as for any formal ceremony. However, if the bride wishes, they may appear in uniform. (The bride generally prefers not to show her title on wedding invitations, although she may; again, see Chapter 5.) If both bride and groom are military officers, all members of the wedding party may wear full dress uniform, with the bride either in a formal wedding dress or her own dress uniform. All other procedures are the same as for any military wedding, including the display of the standards of the bride's military unit.

The Double Wedding

Any two sisters, close relatives, or good friends may wish to express their fondness by sharing their wedding day—with, of course, a savings, both emotional and financial, for their parents. What's more, double weddings can be quite splendid with their multiplicity of attendants, and usually, large number of guests.

A double wedding is most often formal, with each couple having their own set of attendants. (The brides may serve as each other's honor attendants, but this is optional.) Both groups of attendants dress in the same degree of formality, in the same or harmonizing colors. The ushers, for example, might all wear the traditional black-and-white formal suits, while one set of maids wear pale lavender, the other deep plum. Or, for a summer ceremony, one couple might dress their ushers in midnight blue, their maids in softest powder blue, while the other chooses a rich brown for the men, a gentle yellow for the women. The brides wear differently styled dresses with trains and veils of about the same length.

Invitations are usually issued jointly (see Chapter 5). The brides are not sisters? Separate invitations may be sent.

If the two brides are sisters, the older one usually takes precedence in the procession and recessional. Otherwise, the order of the ceremony and the seating arrangements must be worked out carefully in advance. Two aisles mean the processions and recessionals may take place simultaneously, one on each side, with each set of parents in the first pew on either side of their couple's aisle. When there is but one aisle, one set of parents may sit in the second pew or both sets may share the first pew. One couple might lead the procession, the other lead the recessional.

With a single aisle, the two grooms walk in together behind the clergy member and take their places side by side, each with his own best man behind him, the future husband of the first bride standing nearer the aisle. Both sets of ushers, paired by height, lead the procession. The bridesmaids, honor attendant, and flower girl of the first bride come next, followed by the bride on her father's arm. The second set of attendants and the second bride follow in similar fashion. At a double wedding of sisters, a brother or other male relative may escort the second bride to the altar, or the father may escort his elder daughter down the aisle and to her groom, then return to fetch his younger daughter. In either case, the father gives both daughters away.

On reaching the head of the aisle, the attendants usually separate so that those of the first bride are on the left, those of the second bride on the right. The two couples stand side by side in front of the wedding official, the first bride on the left. In a wedding of sisters, the father stands behind the older bride until he gives her away, then moves over to give his younger daughter away before he takes his seat. The ceremony may be divided into sections, with each couple completing each section in turn: first, one couple speaks their vows, then the other. However, the final blessing may be given to both at the same time. Then the two couples may kiss and turn to face their guests.

The recessional is led by the two couples, one before the other, followed by the two sets of honor attendants, then the bridesmaids and ushers in pairs. When the brides have served as each other's honor attendants, the best men escort bridesmaids up the aisle, with the extra ushers bringing up the rear.

A joint reception, which may be especially large and lavish, always follows a double wedding. Sisters receive in the same line, with the older bride and her husband preceding the younger. The honor attendants may participate, but bridesmaids may be excused in order to keep the line to a manageable length. Fathers seldom participate, choosing instead to mingle with and greet their guests. When the brides are not sisters, each family may form a separate receiving line, including the bridesmaids if they wish.

The size of the wedding party and the available space determine whether it's better to have a joint table or separate ones. Each bride may wish to have her own cake, to be cut at the same time. Any imprinted favors or napkins may include the names of both couples and the date, or they may be ordered separately for each couple.

Candlelight Ceremonies

When the wedding will take place in the late afternoon or evening, and the church is a relatively dark one, a candlelight ceremony can be beautiful. Meeting the proper church authorities very early in the planning stage, however, is most important. Local fire regulations may dictate the number and placement of the candles, and the secretary (sexton or verger) should be able to inform you of your limitations as well as the possibilities. Dimming the electrical lighting, for example, may enhance the mood of the setting, but then special spot lighting at the altar may be required for the clergy to see.

Placement of candles to shine throughout the church should be carefully considered—you'll want to keep them out of drafts from air conditioning as well as from natural breezes. Large candles on stands, perhaps decorated by the florist along a seasonal theme (green boughs and red ribbon at holiday time) or with the classic white flowers and satin bows, may be placed at the end of the pew. Another group of candles can define the area where you and your groom will exchange vows.

Acolytes, a pair of responsible boys or girls who are either special friends or regular assistants at the church, might proceed slowly up the aisle, lighting these candles well before the procession is to begin. They often wear the white vestments-over-skirts of the church, and should take their instructions from the officiating clergymember or his or her designate. It is less ceremonial but perhaps more practical for the ushers to make certain the candles are already glowing as guests arrive.

Added drama will come as your attendants make their way down the aisle, to a very slow wedding march. They will bear lighted candles, perhaps sprigged with flowers at the base. The florist can provide holders that are easy to grip. Or, for a charming touch—not to mention safety's sake—the bridesmaids may carry hurricane lamps or old-fashioned lanterns that radiate a soft peach aura.

Candles may also take on symbolic meaning at the ceremony. Two candles might flicker during the service—one on the bride's side of the church, the other on the groom's. A taller candle can stand unlit in the center until the clergy pronounces the couple husband and wife. Then the bride and groom may carry their respective candles to kindle the one in the center, indicating the joining of their families.

Once the recessional has occurred and before the ushers direct the guests to depart, the acolytes might return to the head of the church, snuffing the candles row by row. This creates a more meditative close to the ceremony than is customary, and guests may reflect as appropriate music is softly played. The church lights may be raised gently before the guests file out. Or the guests may walk quietly out under the candleglow.

Any acolytes, of course, should be thanked with a gift or tip, if appropriate.

The Wedding at Home

Your own home, or that of a close relative or friend, provides an especially warm setting for your wedding. An attractive fireplace or a large floral screen will provide an appropriate background for a religious ceremony, with an altar table and kneeling bench brought in if necessary. Formal seating is not required, but you may wish to provide chairs for guests. Chairs are usually arranged on either side of an "aisle" formed by looped ribbons or ropes of flowers and greens.

Your mother or a close friend usually greets guests at the door and directs them to the wedding area: "So glad to see you, Mrs. Kampenga! It looks as though you were able to follow Audrey's directions out here—now for more directions. Just through that hall and to your right. We'll all be gathering in the living room. And if you'd like to freshen up, the bathroom is straight upstairs." Your honor attendant (who is also responsible for greeting the wedding official and showing him or her where to change) may assist. The groom's parents may mingle with the guests before the ceremony, or wait with their son and the best man until they take their places. Ushers are not customary, but a few male relatives or close friends of the groom should be designated to alert guests when the ceremony is about to begin and to escort the groom's parents and your mother to their places near the altar.

The procession is a modified form of the traditional one, with the bridesmaids, honor attendant, and the bride with her father making their entrance from an adjoining room or down a staircase. Or you may enter alone, with your father meeting you at the foot of the stairs or at the entrance to the wedding room, and escorting you to your groom's side.

At the end of the ceremony, your groom will kiss you right away—to make sure no one breaks the tradition of his being the very first to kiss you, his wife! The two of you then turn to receive the hugs and good wishes of your guests. A recessional is not necessary, nor is a receiving line unless you've a great many guests. Instead, you'll simply speak briefly with everyone, then lead the way to the reception area.

The Outdoor Wedding

A large and blooming garden at home is a favorite site for outdoor weddings, from very formal to informal. Procedures are similar to those for any other wedding at home. Pick the prettiest garden spot for the ceremony—before a trellis of fragrant roses, in a latticed summerhouse at the end of a pebbled garden path, beside a sparkling pool. Consult your florist for more ideas. Create an aisle with flowered standards or garlands of greens and, if your dress has a train, spread out a canvas to protect it. The procession is the customary one, omitting ushers unless you've also set up chairs for the seating of guests. And you may do without the recessional entirely. Instead, you and your groom turn to greet your guests immediately after the kiss. You and your parents may form a receiving line, or mingle with your guests, talking to each one individually. Then you retire to the shade of a nearby tent or grove of trees for refreshments.

Other popular outdoor sites include parks and meadows, beaches, and public forests. Check to see if a permit is required for your chosen site and make sure guests know how to get there (send a map with the invitations if you think it's necessary). If parking is limited, arrange for transportation by bus or "shuttle cars" from the nearest large parking area. If you are not near a house but you expect the celebration to go on for more than an hour—as most do—you will have to arrange access to rest rooms for the guests.

When planning any outdoor wedding or reception, you'll be wise to prepare alternative possibilities (moving the wedding inside or renting a large tent for shelter) in case of rain or bad weather on the wedding day. You might even enclose a small card with the invitation, giving this kind of information: "In the event of rain/the wedding will be held/at/Woodington Towne Hall."

The Older Bride

No matter what the age of the bride—forty, fifty, sixty—her wedding is a time for celebration. She and the groom may issue the invitations and announcements themselves or ask a sponsor to do so (see Chapter 5). She will delight in wearing a long dress in a lovely shade of white, marrying in church with attendants at her side, and being escorted down the aisle by her father, brother, or other man of her choice. She may choose not to be given away, however, and she frequently avoids the most elaborate dress and headpiece styles in favor of elegant simplicity: a classic silk shirtwaist in softest ecru, perhaps with a delicately veiled hat.

A large and festive reception is always in order, complete with dancing, toasts, and wedding cake. After having lived on their own many years, the couple, of course, may pay for the party themselves. The mature couple often do without such touches as throwing the bouquet and garter, though they certainly may do so if they wish.

The Wedding of a Member of the Clergy

When the groom is a member of the clergy, the ceremony usually takes place in the bride's church or synagogue with her minister or rabbi officiating. If the bride is a parishioner of the groom's, his superior or another member of the clergy of equal rank might perform the ceremony, frequently with the entire congregation invited. The bride wears a dress suitable to the formality of the wedding, while the groom may be married in his clerical clothes, in formal attire with a clerical collar, or in regular formal dress. The customs of his denomination and the formality of the wedding determine these details.

When the bride is the minister or rabbi, similar procedures are followed. The ceremony is held at her place of worship, with the official of her choice performing the ceremony. She may wear either her clerical garb or a traditional wedding dress appropriate to the style of the wedding.

If one of your parents is a member of the clergy, he or she may officiate at your ceremony. If it's your father, another male relative may escort you down the aisle, your mother step forward to give you away.

The Civil Ceremony

Most civil ceremonies are quiet and intimate ceremonies performed in a courthouse, a judge's chambers, or the home of a justice of the peace. The usual guidelines for an informal wedding apply, with the bride and groom dressing in their best street attire and having only one attendant each. A small reception at the ceremony site, at home, or in a restaurant may follow—and because the very closest family and friends are on hand, it will be an especially warm occasion.

One popular variation is for a couple to marry at a civil ceremony during the day—even exchanging vows they have written themselves—then invite a crowd to a gala reception at night. In this case, the couple would need two outfits—the bride, for example, wearing a suit during the day and changing to a sophisticated cocktail-length or dance-length dress for evening.

If it is a large civil ceremony performed at home or in a club or ballroom, procedures are the same as for a religious ceremony of like formality. Aisles may be formed between rows of chairs for guests, and the wedding party enter in the standard procession. The reception usually begins immediately after the ceremony, at the same location.

Reaffirming the Wedding Vows

Couples who have eloped or married in civil ceremonies for the sake of convenience may ask their clergy to fashion a special blessing or renewal-of-vows ceremony at any time. When such a service is planned shortly after the wedding itself, announcements may be sent and a post-wedding party given. The couple need not expect gifts in this case, but if they receive them from thoughtful friends and relatives, the gifts should, of course, be enjoyed and accepted with the most gracious thanks.

It is becoming more and more common for husbands and wives who have been married quite a while to reaffirm their wedding vows. The occasion might be a wedding anniversary. The couple can repeat the same vows they spoke so long ago or write new ones that express the way their feelings for one another have grown. For example: "We have lived and loved as we promised long ago in the presence of God, and our past and our future are a circle unbroken . . . like this ring, with which I renew my pledge to you of neverending devotion." The service might resemble a wedding before a congregation in church, with the children included this time. Or the clergy can visit the couple's home for a private ceremony. Afterward, a gala party is certainly in order. (See Chapter 5 for wordings of announcements and invitations for such occasions.) The possibilities for a reaffirmation of vows are as endless as for the wedding itself.

Whatever will make the celebration of your marriage special, ingenuity and a little more advance planning than usual will ensure that it's a smooth-running experience for all—especially for the two of you!

11
Remarriage

The real purpose of etiquette has always been—and will always be—to help people feel comfortable and good about themselves. The "rules" and guidelines change as people change. Therefore, many of the traditional differences between a bride's first marriage and her subsequent ones are no longer observed. More important than agonizing over whether or not you can wear white (you can!) is bringing feelings of pleasure and happiness to all the members of your wedding community—you, your groom, your families, and your friends. This chapter is designed to help you and your groom consider your options and choose just the right ceremony and reception for you.

Announcing Your Engagement

If you have children from a previous marriage, you'll probably want to tell them first. How you do so depends largely on their ages and on their relationship with your groom. If they know him well and are used to seeing the two of you together, the news probably will not come as a surprise. Once you've told them privately, you may want to plan some "new family" time together when you can all discuss your future. Every child will have legitimate questions and concerns about this proposed change in his life—"Where will we live?" "What do I call him?" "Do you love him more than me?" even in the case of divorce, "Who is my real father now?" Positive, straightforward answers to these questions will make the adjustment period easier for all.

Let your parents in on the good news next. And, if you do have children, your former spouse and his parents should also be notified. Then spread the word among your friends and family. Women who have been widowed or who have been divorced may enjoy having a new engagement ring to show everyone—and in deference to their new commitment, it should be the only ring they wear on the left hand until the wedding day.

Traditionally, no formal announcement of a "second-time" bride's engagement is made (only the wedding is reported). You may, however, submit the news to your local paper if you wish (see Chapter 1).

Should it be your first marriage, but your groom's second, your parents may announce the engagement as is customary.

Pre-Wedding Parties

A second-time bride usually doesn't receive quite as lavish a round of parties as she did for her first marriage. But your friends may still wish to host an informal shower (perhaps with both men and women attending), your parents or other close relatives may hold a dinner in your honor, and you may even wish to give a cocktail party or brunch in your own home. Certainly, where there are children involved (yours or his or both), you'll want to plan a number of special get-togethers where you can all get better acquainted. Some of these might well include friends of you both so the children can see how the two of you function as a couple as well as parents.

However your friends choose to salute your wedding, your response is always equally warm—delighted verbal thanks followed up with a written note and perhaps a small gift of flowers for the hostess.

Planning Your Ceremony

Traditionally, a second-time bride avoids a very formal ceremony in favor of a semiformal or informal wedding for close friends and family only. But if you missed a big wedding the first time or want very much to walk down the aisle in a long white dress escorted by someone close, you may. Just be sure to share your plans with your parents so they can tactfully inform the rest of your family. That way your most conservative guests won't be surprised on wedding day.

You and your groom should certainly have honor attendants and, if you invite more than fifty guests, ushers as well. Bridesmaids are frequently omitted, but if you or your groom have children, you may ask them to participate. It's an especially thoughtful way of including them in the wedding. A teenage daughter might serve as your attendant, teenage boys might usher, younger children may be flower girls, ring bearers, or pages. If you plan a very small ceremony, you may simply ask your children to stand with you at the altar to share more fully in the wedding ceremony; they might read a special poem or prayer, even escort you down the aisle together. But when children express a preference not to participate, it's best not to insist. And always check with the child's other parent before proceeding with plans.

The smallest wedding you can plan—and the one most traditional—is the civil ceremony with just the two of you and your attendants. It might take place at city hall, in a judge's chambers, or at your or your parents' home. You might plan a small religious ceremony at a chapel, church rectory, or home. The guest list is traditionally limited to your and your groom's immediate family and closest friends, although you may, of course, include everyone and marry on a grander scale at a large hall, club, or church. If you have remained close to your former in-laws, you may wish to invite them as well. But you are not obligated to do so, nor are they expected to attend.

Many second-time brides find the most appealing plan involves a small, intimate ceremony followed by a large, fun-filled reception complete with champagne, dancing, and wedding cake. This way you can include everyone you love in your wedding celebration without risk of offending parents or relatives who may find a large ceremony inappropriate.

A groom's previous marriages seldom affect his wedding.

Visiting Your Clergy or Judge

As soon as you've decided on the size and type of ceremony you'd like, make an appointment for you and your groom to visit your minister, rabbi, priest, or other ceremony official. While many restrictions on the remarriage of divorced persons have been eased in recent years, you may still need not only your own clergy's permission but, in some cases, permission from higher church authorities as well.

In addition to setting the date and time, discuss all your plans for the ceremony: music, flowers, attendants, and the like. Your ceremony official may have his or her own suggestions—the use of the chapel rather than the main church, religious rather than secular music, special roles for your children. If for any reason the clergy of your own congregation are reluctant to perform the ceremony of your choice, it's best to find out early while you still have time to seek another ceremony official. Ask other remarried friends for suggestions, or call local churches.

Invitations and Announcements

The bride and groom may issue their own invitations for a small, informal ceremony. Send brief notes or telephone your closest friends and relatives. When more than fifty guests are invited, you may choose to mail printed invitations, using this wording:

The pleasure of your company
is requested at the marriage of
Mrs. Marcia Maureen Craig (or, for a widow,
Mrs. Albert Brendon Craig)
to
Mr. Nathan Randolph Carter
Saturday, the fourth of May
at four o'clock
Hotel Mark Hopkins
San Francisco

R.S.V.P.
1053 Shady Lane
Oakland, California 12345

The "Mrs." and "Mr." before first names may be omitted if the bride and groom prefer. (If the bride's parents issue the invitations, they use the appropriate wording described in Chapter 5.)

No matter how small the ceremony, the reception following may be as large as desired, with printed invitations issued by the bride and groom or by their parents. When a large reception follows a small ceremony, you might send formal reception invitations to all your guests with handwritten ceremony cards inserted for those who are invited to both.

Formal announcements sent after the ceremony frequently prove an excellent way to notify friends of your marriage. Your parents may "have the honour of announcing" your marriage, or you and your groom may send your own announcements reading:

Mrs. Marcia Maureen Craig (or, Mrs. Albert Brendon Craig)
and
Mr. Nathan Randolph Carter
announce their marriage
Saturday, the fourth of May
One thousand nine hundred and eighty-one
San Francisco

All printed invitations and announcements may, of course, have the traditional look or a personalized design. Some brides with children issue their invitations in their children's names or announce the formation of a "new family," perhaps including a photograph of the bride and groom with all their offspring.

If you wish, you may also send an announcement to your local newspaper, including all the details of the marriage but omitting descriptions of the ceremony, your dress, and the like. Such an announcement might read:

Marcia Maureen Craig and Nathan Randolph Carter, both of Oakland, were married Saturday, May fourth, at the Hotel Mark Hopkins in San Francisco by Justice James Howard of the California State Supreme Court. The bride is the daughter of Mr. and Mrs. Daniel Ackerman of Los Angeles. She is employed by the University of California. Mr. Carter is the son of Mrs. Leon Ball Carter and the late Mr. Carter of San Francisco. He is an accountant with the firm of Richardson and Level. Mrs. Craig's previous marriage was terminated by divorce. The couple will reside in Berkeley.

If you wish to include details of your ceremony or reception, check with the society editor regarding the requirements or read similar stories in the newspaper.

The Question of Names

In the past, a woman who had been divorced used a combination of her maiden and married surnames (Mrs. White Smith) in any formal context. Today, it is common for her to use her given names and married surname (Barbara Lynn Smith) or her first name, maiden name, and married name (Barbara White Smith). Widows can, of course, go by their husband's first and last names (Mrs. Robert Herman), but may also prefer their given first name and married last name. When you remarry, you'll have the option of dropping your former married surname in favor of your new husband's name, creating a combination of the two, or keeping the name you are known by now.

If you have already established a professional reputation under your maiden name or your first married name, you may wish to keep that name for all business uses, taking your new husband's name for social use only. Or, as is happening more often these days, you may wish to simply keep your name as it is now (especially if you and your children share a common last name). Another alternative is to drop your maiden name and retain your first married name to help in identification. Thus, if you have been known as Barbara Lynn Smith, you may now wish to go by Barbara Smith Jones.

Wedding Dress

Romantically lacy, long, and white or traditionally elegant, street-length, ecru or pastel—the second-time bride has more choice in wedding dress today than ever before. Depending on the formality of the ceremony and the time of day, a second-time bride may wear anything from a simple, cream-colored suit with a neat, matching cloche to a long, ruffly dress in white or her favorite color. She may wear her flowers or carry a bouquet or flower-trimmed prayer book. She might complete her wedding look with a dramatic picture hat, a wreath of fresh or silk flowers. The only thing you might do without is the veil—long a symbol of virginity. Aside from the type of ceremony you plan, other factors you'll want to consider include your age, the circumstances of your first marriage, your groom's wishes, and the feelings of your family or clergy.

Once you've decided on your wedding style, the rest of the wedding party follows suit. Your honor attendant, any bridesmaids, and the mothers choose dresses in the same length and of a style similar to your own. The men may wear traditional formal clothes if you wear a long wedding dress. For a semiformal or informal wedding, they wear dark suits, white shirts, and dark four-in-hand ties. Children wear party dresses or suits as for any formal wedding.

The Ceremony

Traditionally, a bride's second wedding is much abbreviated, with neither a procession nor a recessional, and only the simplest decorations and most subtle music. The bride and her honor attendant enter the church or chapel through the vestry door to meet the groom and his best man, already waiting at the altar. After the ceremony, the couple turn to greet their guests. At a civil ceremony—in a judge's chamber, perhaps—decorations and music are usually omitted, but the procedure is similar, with the bride and her attendant entering the room to find the groom and his best man waiting.

A larger, more formal ceremony for a second-time bride today might include a small procession with the bride escorted by her father, her son, or another close family friend or relative. A woman who has been divorced is rarely given away a second time, but a widow may ask a brother, son, or her father to escort her down the aisle and give her away. The traditional recessional would, in this case, follow the ceremony.

If a second-time bride wishes to include bridesmaids and ushers in her wedding party, she may certainly plan a regular procession and recessional. Just be sure to discuss plans with the ceremony official in advance.

The Reception

Neither the bride's nor the groom's previous marriages has any effect on the size or the style or the reception. Make it as extravagant a party as you wish, complete with all the wedding traditions—receiving line, dancing, wedding cake, and champagne. You might omit such first-wedding customs as tossing the bride's bouquet and garter, the white cake decorated with tiny bride and groom, and the exit through a shower of rice. Instead, consider icing or trimming your cake with a pretty pastel and garnishing it with fresh flowers, have guests line up to wave and call good wishes as you leave for your honeymoon.

You and your groom may head up the receiving line yourselves while your parents circulate among the guests. And, since some guests will not be giving you gifts, it's best (and safest) to avoid any package-opening ceremony. Otherwise, your reception may follow all the procedures for a first wedding, including the "first dance," the ceremonial cutting of the cake, and rounds of toasts from your parents, honor attendants, and friends.

If you or your groom have children, you may want to make a special effort to include them in the reception fun—perhaps planning your ceremony for afternoon instead of evening so they'll be wide awake, offering them special seats of honor at the bride's table, even (for a very small wedding party) letting them be the ones to choose a favorite restaurant as the reception site.

Wedding Gifts

As a second-time bride, you'll probably receive fewer gifts than you did for your first wedding, though many of your close friends and family will send presents. If it's the groom's second marriage, his friends are not expected to send gifts, but they frequently do. Gift preferences may be registered at stores.

A first-time bride, even though her groom has been married before, will receive gifts from most of her guests and may display them (as described in Chapter 16).

Written thank-you notes must be sent to everyone who offers a gift, just as for a first wedding.

Who Pays for What

If it is a second marriage for both bride and groom, the groom may assume all costs or the couple may split them. There are many ways to divide the costs, depending on the financial status of each partner. Some popular methods are to assign expenses in advance (she pays for her dress, the flowers, the cake; he pays for the church, the reception site, the champagne); to have one person pay for the ceremony expenses, the other for the reception; or simply pay bills as they come up, then total receipts after the wedding and reimburse the person who paid more.

If it is the bride's first marriage, or if she is a very young widow or divorcée, her parents may offer to pay for the wedding. Or, if the couple are not yet in a financial position to pay for the wedding, either set of parents may offer to assist them and the couple may accept if they wish.

Sometimes couples find that they must choose between a lavish ceremony and a large reception. You'll have to decide which is more important to you. One thing you should try not to skimp on, however, is your honeymoon. Make sure you get away for at least a few days; you'll certainly need the rest and relaxation after the exciting but nonetheless exhausting events surrounding your wedding. And surely some time spent together—just the two of you, away from family and friends—is a perfect way to begin a new marriage.

12
Your Reception

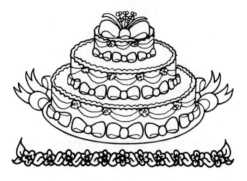

A buffet that seems never to end, the band with the best beat in town, a night full of hugs and kisses and maybe even a few happy tears. Is that the wedding reception you have in mind? Or do you look forward to something more casual, more intimate—just you two, your parents, and a few close friends crowded into a booth at your favorite inn, enjoying the specialty of the house. As long as it affords your friends and family an opportunity to greet you and wish you well, your wedding reception may be either of the above—or anything in between. Champagne, punch, or another beverage suitable for toasting the future, along with some kind of wedding cake are the only things you really need.

You may hold your reception at home or in the garden, at a private club or a church hall, at a large ballroom or at a restaurant. Serve punch and cake, cocktails and hors d'oeuvres, or imported champagne and a five-course meal. Make it a breakfast, a luncheon, or an afternoon tea. Even when your budget is limited, a simple reception for all your guests may add more to your wedding pleasure than the most elaborate feast for only a few.

Reception Timetable

Here's a schedule for the most common kind of wedding reception, a light buffet for two hundred, lasting about three hours. If you are having a more lavish menu or inviting guests who love to party, then you must of course, allow more time. Do adjust this timetable to your plans.

The reception is about to begin: Cars arrive at the reception site with bride, groom, and all the members of the wedding party.

The first half hour: The bridal party forms the receiving line and guests begin to pass by. Drinks are poured as guests mingle. If there are table-seating cards, guests may pick them up now.

After one hour: The buffet is announced, and the members of the wedding party are seated at the bride's table. The guests line up for the buffet, while the members of the wedding party are served at their own table. At this point, the best man will rise to propose the first toast to the bride and groom. The groom may return the best man's toast, then toast the bride, his parents, and his new in-laws. Although not traditional, the bride may follow suit. After all the toasting is finished, the musicians resume playing.

After one and one-half hours: The first course is cleared from the head table. The musicians strike up the dance music, and the "first dance" begins. The other traditional dances follow, then the rest of the guests may join in the dancing.

After two hours: The tables are cleared of food, and the musicians signal it is time for the cake-cutting ceremony. Maids and ushers line up on either side of the table while the rest of the guests gather round to watch. The bride and groom cut and share the first slice, then give each other's parents their pieces. The cake is served to the guests.

The last half hour: The single women all cluster in a convenient spot, and the bride throws her bouquet. The bride's garter may then be tossed to a group of assembled bachelors, although this is optional. Then the bride and groom slip away to change into their going-away clothes and return to say good-bye to their parents. They run out to their car in a shower of rice—and they're off on a fun-filled honeymoon. When the parents are ready to leave, they signal the musicians to stop playing and for the bar to close. They then bid farewell to all their guests.

Incidentally, it may be wise to appoint a very close friend or couple to handle the schedule, should any snag have to be discussed with the caterer or banquet manager. This relieves the father of the bride to see to the wedding guests. These special people should be pointed out to the caterer and identified with corsages or boutonnières, and thanked after the wedding with a personal note from the bride's parents.

The Receiving Line

Your mother, as hostess, is the first to greet guests, followed in order by your groom's mother, his father, you, your groom, and the maid or matron of honor. If your father wishes to join the line, he stands between the two mothers. He may, however, prefer to circulate among the guests as usually done, and the groom's father today may do the same.

The best man, the ushers, and child attendants do not participate in the line. Bridesmaids may, but in the interests of keeping the receiving line short at a very large reception, they may help get the party going with the guests instead.

If you have no mother or stepmother to receive your guests, your father may stand at the head of the line with your grandmother, a sister, or an aunt. When the reception is hosted by persons other than the bride's parents, they are the first in line to meet the guests. If you are hosting your own reception, of course, you and your groom stand at the head of the line.

Set up the line in a convenient spot near the entrance where guests can move down it easily, then go on past the bride's book, and directly into refreshment area (traditionally held at the reception, the line can be at the ceremony site so it doesn't hold up the party). At a large reception with a long line, champagne, ice water, or another cool beverage may be served to guests waiting in line, and a few chairs placed nearby for those who become fatigued.

All the women in the line may wear their hats and gloves, but men should remove theirs. You might hold your bouquet in your left hand, or set it aside to show your new gleaming wedding band. The bridesmaids, if they participate, always keep their flowers in the left hand.

Guests going along the line are introduced to each person in turn, and move quickly on to allow room for those behind them. Your mother, for example, might start with, "Celia, I'd love you to meet Gene's mother, Rosemary Hart." As your mother shakes hands with the next guest, your groom's mother says a brief word. Then you might announce, "Aunt Celia, here's Gene. Gene, her family, the Rangers, are the ones who sent those terrific balloon wine glasses." Now, your groom: "Your glasses are *my* size—thank you! Celia Rangers, have you met Jill's maid of honor and college roommate, Andrea Shields?" The idea is to keep con-

THE RECEIVING LINE: 1) Mother of the Bride, 2) Mother of the Groom, 3) Father of the Groom (optional), 4) Bride, 5) Groom, 6) Bride's Honor Attendant, 7) Bridesmaids (optional).

versation short, but still give some small fact that will help people remember one another. Although you precede your groom in line, he may reach out to introduce you to his own relatives and friends. After the last guest has been welcomed, you two may move to take your seats at the head table, or to cut the cake or start the dancing.

Seating Arrangements

The focus of the reception room is, of course, the bride's table, where all the members of the wedding party are seated. The table, which may be of any shape, is sometimes elevated on a dais. It's usually covered with a pretty, long cloth of white lace, damask, or linen fabric. Make certain the decorations are low—bouquets and candles or garlands of flowers, greens, and ribbons—so that the guests' view of you and the bridal party are not obstructed. Unless the table is round, seating is usually on one side only, with you and your groom in the center, bridesmaids and ushers in alternating seats on either side (see sketch). Attendants who are married to each other, however, need not sit together.

When the wedding party is a small one, the husbands and wives of married attendants, your parents, and the officiating authority (and spouse or assistant, if any) may join the bride's table. Otherwise, there is a separate parents' table with your mother and father in the places for hosts at opposite ends. The groom's father sits at your mother's right, the wedding official at her left, the groom's mother sits at your father's right, the wedding official's spouse or assistant at his left. These are the places of honor. You may also arrange two parents' tables, one for your parents, one for your groom's, so that more relatives and friends may be among those given a seat at the parents' tables. If your parents or your groom's are divorced, they may appreciate separate tables to share with their own parents and relatives. At the reception following a Jewish wedding, the parents and grandparents of the bride and groom, the rabbi, the cantor, and their spouses may be seated at the bridal table, and the bridesmaids and ushers seated among the other guests.

White cards mark each place at the bride's and parents' tables, but are optional elsewhere. Guests may be left free to find their own places with special friends, or you may do a complete seating plan and designate each place, putting people together who haven't met yet but might enjoy doing so. In this case, you may want to have table numbers on cards placed near the entrance to tell each guest where to look for his seat. It's also a nice surprise for guests to find a pretty favor—such as lace-wrapped almonds, or candle tagged with your names and wedding date—at their places. A special table for children, with games and books available after the meal and a pair of teenagers to supervise, may be appreciated by parents who wish to enjoy your reception without having to worry about what their youngsters are up to.

THE BRIDE'S TABLE: 1) Bride, 2) Groom, 3) Bride's Honor Attendant, 4) Best Man, 5) Bridesmaids, 6) Ushers.

Refreshments

A wedding reception should always include a wedding cake and a beverage suitable for drinking to your happiness. Champagne is traditional, contributing to the overall "special occasion" feeling. Champagne is appropriate at any hour, and you may serve it during the entire reception or only for toasts. Ginger ale, white grape juice, or any punch may be substituted for champagne, but coffee, tea, and water are not generally used for toasts. Therefore, tea receptions usually offer a choice of alcoholic or nonalcoholic punch. Champagne punch and mixed drinks are popular in many areas as well.

All daytime wedding receptions were once called "breakfasts," but the term is rarely used today. After a morning wedding, however, you might still serve a real breakfast: perhaps cooling fresh fruit, shirred eggs, hot sausages, and muffins. Luncheon fare (a light soup, creamy chicken casserole, and broiled tomatoes) complements a high noon wedding.

Ceremonies starting between one and four in the afternoon are typically followed by a tea or cocktail reception featuring light nibbles like open-faced sandwiches, nuts, and mints, or a buffet of hot and cold hors d'oeuvres. A hot buffet or a seated dinner of at least three courses is the most common follow-up to an evening wedding. Your caterer or banquet manager will help you plan the menu and advise you on the quantities needed. It is most courteous, of course, to serve guests the amount of food they would expect at that hour and smart to time your wedding accordingly. If you are trying to cut costs and wish to offer only champagne and cake, for example, you might better plan a wedding at two o'clock in the afternoon than at noon when guests will be hungry for lunch.

Your Wedding Cake

Even if your wedding is attended only by two witnesses and

your parents, you'll probably want to celebrate with a cake. It's been an important part of weddings since Roman days.

The familiar frothy white confection topped with fresh flowers, sugar wedding bells, or similar ornaments is called the *bride's cake*. It's usually several layers or tiers of light pound, sponge, or white cake, although any flavor (including chocolate or spice) may be chosen. Because tradition has it that a piece of the bride's cake under a single woman's pillow will lead her to dream of her future husband, it's customary to cut the cake and serve it at the reception, with extra slices provided for guests to take home. Napkins or tiny boxes might be supplied to those who wish to take pieces of cake with them. If you won't be having a groom's cake, do freeze the top layer of the bride's cake to share on your first anniversary.

The less familiar groom's cake is a dark, rich fruitcake, frequently iced to match and used as the top layer of the bride's cake. Seal the groom's cake in a tin with brandy (as you would a holiday fruitcake) to eat on your anniversaries. Or make this cake the one you'll pack in individual boxes to distribute to your guests as favors.

Give your wedding cake the spotlight (and keep it safe from accidental jostling) on a separate table, covered by a white cloth and trimmed with flowers or greens.

You'll cut the wedding cake just before dessert at a luncheon or dinner reception, just after guests have been received at a tea or cocktail reception. Your groom places his right hand over yours and together you cut into the bottom layer with a ribbon-tied silver knife. The bride and groom traditionally share the first slice as a symbol of their willingness to share each other's household from then on. It is a loving gesture for the bride to give her new in-laws their pieces after that, then the groom to serve his. The rest of the cake is then cut (by a friend designated in advance or by a member of the caterer's staff) and served to the guests.

Dancing

Although dancing is not necessary, it does add a happy, festive note to any wedding reception. An orchestra is nice, but a string trio, a piano, or even a stereo will do also. (See Chapter 13.) At a hotel or club reception, the area in front of the bride's table is usually cleared for the dancing. At home, you might set aside one whole room or have a temporary dance floor laid down at the end of a large living room. For a garden reception, guests may dance on the terrace or on a temporary floor set up under a tent or over a pool.

You and your husband will want to lead off the dancing, circling the floor alone to your favorite tune. You are claimed by your father next, while the groom dances with his new mother-in-law. The best man and the father of the groom dance with you after that, while the groom dances with your honor attendant and his own mother. The order of these traditional dances is optional, but they are usually completed before the guests join in. (It's not necessary to dance through an entire song.)

At a very large reception, you may want guests to begin dancing as soon as they've been through the receiving line and the music begins. Your father might see to it that this happens. Then, after you've caught your breath from greeting guests, the musicians signal everyone to clear the floor with a pause in the music or an arresting fanfare and you and your groom begin the traditional first dance. You'll probably dance with each usher; your groom, with each bridesmaid before the dancing ends. It is also customary for each man in the wedding party to request a dance with bridesmaids and both mothers.

Toasts

Toasts to and from the happy couple add to the celebratory feeling of every wedding reception. They may begin any time after the receiving line has ended and everyone has been served a glass of champagne or other bubbly beverage. The best man always proposes the first toast. He may word it any way he likes. And he may follow the two steps in proposing any toast: include a reference to your relationship to the person or persons being honored, and add a thought about their future good fortune. The best man might, therefore, say: "Here's to Sharon and Gary. I wanted to come to their wedding so much, I introduced them! May their lives be full of the kind of happiness we are enjoying here today." When the best man has completed his toast, everyone except you and your groom rises and drinks to it.

The groom usually responds with thanks to his best man and a toast or two of his own—to you, to his parents, or to his new in-laws. You might then rise to offer your own toast: "To my husband, the most wonderful man in the world. To my new family, with thanks for raising such a wonderful man. And to my parents, for all the love and strength they've given me. May we all have many, many more memorable days together." Other members of the wedding party may then propose additional toasts if they wish. All those present, except the person being toasted, should raise their glasses to each toast. At the end of the toasts, the best man may read aloud any congratulatory telegrams or letters sent by absent friends and relatives.

Throwing the Bouquet and Garter

Just before you leave to change into your going-away clothes, word is passed to the bridesmaids and other single women to gather at the bottom of a stairway, under a balcony, or at some other convenient spot. If your going-away flowers are part of your bridal bouquet, remove them first. If you've carried a prayer book instead of a bouquet, you may toss the floral decoration and ribbon streamers. If you've had a large cascade of long-stemmed flowers or wish to save your own bouquet, you may toss a token bouquet made up by your florist especially for this purpose.

Some brides turn and throw the bouquet over a shoulder, but if you'd like to aim at your sister or a dear friend, you may want to face the group as you throw. Tradition says that the woman who catches the bouquet will be the next to marry.

There is another light-hearted tradition that may be observed, but only if the bride wishes. Her garter, most likely of blue satin, may be thrown to the ushers and other bachelors. The groom removes it from your leg, then, according to local custom, you or your groom may toss it, with the man who captures it destined to be the next to wed.

Planning Two Receptions

If you and your groom live in a city far away from your parents' homes, or if your groom's hometown is a long way from your own, you may wish to marry at one location, then hold a second reception later at the other for all the friends and family who did not travel to the wedding—including those of a divorced parent not with you that day. Such a reception may be similar to the first, with printed invitations issued by your or your groom's parents (see Chapter 5), a wedding cake and champagne or punch, flowers, dancing, and another round of toasts.

More commonly, such a reception is simply a large cocktail party or buffet, hosted by the two of you with friends and relatives just enjoying themselves and wishing you well. The receiving line, bouquet and garter toss, and shower of rice may then be omitted, and invitations are often informal notes or telephone calls. If you are planning this party from a long distance, do engage the help of friends or relatives who can help find a suitable location, hire a caterer, and generally organize the festivities. Thank them with a gift of flowers or a special memento similar to those you gave your wedding attendants.

Your groom's parents may also wish to host you at a reception for their hometown friends. They may issue printed invitations (again, see Chapter 5), and stand in a receiving line with the two of you to greet guests. A champagne toast from your father-in-law to you, and one from you or your groom to his parents would be appropriate. Otherwise the reception may be the same as for any other party at the time and season.

Leaving the Reception

When the toasting's done, the cake's been cut, the bouquet thrown, you and your groom will slip away to change, then depart in the traditional shower of rice. (Young children or friends may distribute pretty packets of rice to guests, which may even contain birdseed if an ecological as well as safe alternative is sought.) In the confusion, don't forget to bid a special farewell to each of your parents. Their happy memories, and yours, will increase in value with every passing year.

13
Wedding Music and Readings

Choosing music you love is one of the most natural ways to add meaning to your wedding. Whether you're planning an elegant cathedral ceremony and a lavish reception or an intimate exchange of vows beside the mantelpiece at home, use music to create a mood of both solemnity and joy for your marriage ceremony and to lend a festive note to your reception. A favorite poem or Bible passage can also personalize your wedding—as much for your guests as for you and your groom.

Music: What and When

For the traditional ceremony at a church or chapel, the music might begin with a soft prelude lasting about half an hour while guests are seated. Just after your mother has been seated is the traditional time for a soloist or choir to sing, or a small ensemble group to perform. You'll certainly want a majestic processional to herald you and your wedding party down the aisle; perhaps another solo after your vows; and, of course, a triumphant recessional. The organist might conclude with a lively postlude as guests file out.

You may choose to trust the church organist's selection of appropriate numbers for the prelude and postlude from the wealth of beautiful music available. Or ask to hear several different possibilities, then pick your favorites. There are so many lovely classical pieces appropriate to the occasion, you might even want to visit the listening room of your local library for several sessions before making your final decision.

The "Bridal Chorus" from *Lohengrin* ("Here Comes the Bride") and the "Wedding March" from Mendelssohn's *Midsummer Night's Dream* are two very popular processional choices. But do consider choosing something with more personal meaning—perhaps the regal "Rigaudon" by André Campra or the exuberant "Bourée" from Handel's *Water Music*. For solos, "Oh, Promise Me" remains ever popular, but you might also choose from current love songs and movie themes, folk and country ballads, classical works, maybe even that "first song" you two ever danced to. Ask your organist, choir director, or a musical friend to suggest some possibilities. Then be sure to listen to every suggestion until you find just the pieces you want. Traditional or contemporary secular (nonreligious) music should, of course, be cleared with the clergy officiating at your service.

There are a number of ways to add your own personal touches via your choice of musicians as well. If you've a string or woodwind quartet, a group of madrigal singers, or a trumpeter in mind to enhance the processional and recessional, ask the church or chapel organist to suggest some names. (But remember, in many areas, you'll have to pay the church organist whether you actually employ him or her, or not.) You might also call local high schools and colleges for the names of string quartets and soloists. Do you want to include the people you love in your wedding plans? If they are professionals, or almost as good, let your Aunt Eleanor play the prelude on the piano and your music-major roommate offer a solo after the vows. Otherwise, they might take the stage at the reception where the mood is lighter. Thinking of singing yourselves? Consider it carefully; even the most seasoned performer can get wedding-day nerves, and it may be most effective for you to simply say your vows with clarity and confidence.

Whoever the musicians, give them plenty of time to practice, make sure you include them in the wedding rehearsal, and pay them promptly—professionals, on the day of the wedding (frequently in cash); friends, with thoughtful gifts, perhaps distributed at the rehearsal dinner.

Music for Protestant Weddings

Usually a Protestant ceremony means you can have both popular and religious music. It is likely to be performed by the church organist, soloist, or choir who will all be familiar with wedding procedures and can offer a wide variety of selections for you to choose from. If you request something out of the ordinary, be sure to allow the musicians plenty of time to learn and practice it.

Music for Catholic Weddings

Some Catholic clergy may ask that you avoid popular music in favor of religious selections and the hymns sung at regular Masses. (To find out, ask.) Sometimes a choir sings; more often, a soloist. "Ave Maria" is probably the favorite, but consider other possibilities like Franck's "Panis Angelicus" and "Ave Verum" by Mozart.

Music for Jewish Weddings

Secular music, including the usual wedding marches, is permitted at many Reform and Conservative weddings, but Orthodox rabbis may prefer you use only traditional Hebrew music. The cantor traditionally chants the Seven Blessings and may perform other solo pieces if requested. Ask the rabbi and the cantor for suggestions on both traditional Hebrew songs and contemporary Israeli music.

Readings for Weddings

Whether you and your groom compose your own poem or prayer to accompany your vows, or choose a verse from another source, a brief reading can express special thoughts you wish to share with the guests at your ceremony. Sources to consider? The Bible (particularly the Song of Solomon), *The Prophet* by Kahlil Gibran, passages from Thoreau, and the works of modern-day inspirational writers like Erich Fromm. Look into anthologies of poetry (especially the Brownings) and the lyrics of popular love songs as well. Do check your clergy or librarian for other ideas. You might include beloved friends or brothers and sisters by asking them to do the reading for you. Natural points for the readings to be offered are before the vows and after the exchange of rings. To follow along, each guest might enjoy having his or her own copy of the reading, perhaps included in a wedding program distributed before the ceremony.

Music for Wedding Receptions

A string trio in the background, a pianist in the corner, a small orchestra on a raised platform, even a stereo or tapes. Music brings a special note of festivity to even the most casual reception.

Choose your musicians as soon as possible and give them a list of your favorites, as well as those of your closest family and friends. A mix of current popular hits and old standards will give everyone from your grandmother to the best man something to hum to. If there'll be dancing, be sure to let the band know how swinging you want the party to get—and which song you want for your "first dance." You may also ask the band leader to help coordinate the rhythm of the reception. He may be able to signal guests when you enter the room (probably with "Here Comes the Bride"), when you're ready to cut the cake, and when you're leaving. Do specify which songs you wish played at each point, especially if you're not fond of "The Bride Cuts the Cake" to the tune of "The Farmer in the Dell."

If there is a song you would like played that is not generally known, an obliging group will gladly take the sheet music from you ahead of time so they can rehearse the tune and play it beautifully just for you.

14
Your Wedding Flowers

A wedding just wouldn't be a wedding without flowers. They bring beauty, color, and a wealth of tradition to marriage ceremonies and receptions, from very formal to informal. Picture now the effect of lush greens at the aisles of a whitewashed chapel, pastel carnations against a dark-paneled altar. Or, rose-filled vases creating an aura of romance at home, flower-touched garlands looping the catering-hall bandstand.

Consult your florist in the early stages of your planning. He or she can advise you on the most appropriate flowers for various uses (if they'll be dancing till the small hours, the mothers will want flowers that look fresh a long time), tell you which will be most readily available at the time of your wedding, and show you samples of the various types and shapes of bouquets as well as dozens of blossoms you've probably never seen or heard of before. The florist might also suggest some attractive arrangements and color schemes to go along with your own ideas. You can have any flowers you like, even out of season, thanks to hot-house growing and air shipping. But in-season flowers—bold chrysanthemums in the fall rather than tender tulips—may cost less and look most natural in your setting.

Wedding Bouquets

The bride and her attendants traditionally carry a bouquet at all but the most informal weddings. It may be anything from an armload of flowers to a small nosegay, but it should be scaled to your size and complement your dress. A loose spill of feathered chrysanthemums, for example, might overpower a petite bride in a street-length dress, but be stunning for a tall bride in a long, flowing look.

The bride's bouquet was traditionally made up of all-white flowers, usually mixed with ivy, the symbol of fidelity, and other greens. Some favorites: white roses, orchids, carnations, steph-anotis, lilies of the valley, and gardenias. But many others are chosen in season. Easter lilies make lovely spring bouquets, sum-mer arrangements frequently include babies' breath or Queen Anne's lace, and white poinsettias look most festive at holiday time. Today, color blended with white or all-color bouquets are also popular choices for brides—they can range from two or three dramatic tiger lilies to a nosegay of bright-hued carnations to a woodsy bundle of yellow freesia.

Be sure to give your florist a complete description of your dress, including a sketch and fabric swatches, if possible, so he or she can recommend an appropriate style for your bouquet. If your waist and skirt are scattered with appliqués, for example, a crescent cascade might mask these pretty details, while a round Colonial clutch of flowers would allow your dress to show. In-cidentally, although the groom customarily pays for the bride's flowers, if it is a formal wedding, the bride still chooses them. (She and her family may also pay for them if this is simpler.)

Afraid you won't want to part with your flowers when it comes time to toss the bouquet? Have a replica made up especially for this purpose. Then you will have the pleasure of hearing someone close to you cry "I've got it!" as well as of keeping yours as a memento.

The bridesmaids and honor attendant usually carry similar arrangements of the same flowers, but the maid or matron of honor frequently has a different shade or a contrasting color to set her apart. It is not necessary for your attendants' bouquets to be duplicates of your own, but they should be a like design. If you plan on whimsical daisies, for example, your bridesmaids might carry daffodils or cornflowers, but not formal orchids. Various colors of roses and carnations are popular for bridesmaids' bouquets the year around, but some of the most attractive arrangements feature seasonal flowers. In spring, your bridesmaids might wear pink dresses and carry dogwood, lilacs, or anemones. Yellow daffodils and forsythia are also pretty. For bridesmaids in a summer wedding: red and white peonies, multicolored sweetpeas, or pink and red larkspur. A fall wedding? Consider russet chrysanthemums mixed with autumn leaves or sheaves of wheat. If you'll be married in December, you might plan a red and white color scheme using poinsettias, roses, or holly. Whatever you choose, be sure to give your florist a complete description of your bridesmaids' dresses and a swatch of fabric to guide him or her in designing appropriate bouquets.

Flower girls traditionally tote baskets of loose petals to be strewn in the bride's path, but remember, this can cause someone to fall. Instead, today's flower girl often carries a miniature bouquet of flowers arranged in a basket, attached to a muff, or fashioned into a nosegay. Rosebuds, violets, lilies of the valley, or other dainty blossoms look very sweet.

Flowers to Wear

The bride at an informal wedding usually chooses flowers for her dress or for her wrist instead of a bouquet. White orchids are popular with many brides, but you may wear any flowers that complement your outfit—even a muff woven of greens and daisies. An informal wedding means you may, should you choose, give the privilege of choosing your flowers to the groom. If you have a formal wedding, the orchid or other flowers from the center of your bouquet can be removed to pin on your going-away clothes. Or you may have your florist make up a fresh arrangement to wear for traveling.

The mothers and grandmothers of the bride and groom are customarily presented with flowers to wear at the wedding. These may be made of any flowers that harmonize with their dresses, but personal preferences should be taken into consideration. Some women, for example, like nothing better than roses, but a mother with her own rose garden may well find a cluster of cymbidium orchids more special for the occasion.

Prayer Book Flowers

In a formal or semiformal wedding, you may carry a flower-covered prayer book instead of a bouquet. This may be a new book purchased for the occasion or an old family Bible or missal. Whether new or old, the book may be covered in white silk or satin to complement your dress. Although you may choose any flowers you like, white orchids, with the addition of a cascade of smaller blossoms or ribbon streamers when the bride wears a long dress, are classic.

Floral Headpieces

Although silk flowers are much more common these days, headpieces made of real orange blossoms or other light flowers are still worn by some brides and bridesmaids. These are usually made in the shape of a crescent that fits across the top of the head or in a circle that sits on the crown. Such headpieces may be attached to a small comb or held in place with hairpins. A veil can be attached to the bride's headpiece but is not necessary for the bridesmaids. Another option is for the bride to wear her headpiece and veil for the ceremony, then change to a few pretty hair flowers for reception dancing.

Boutonnières

The groom and every man in the wedding party—the best man, ushers, and fathers—traditionally wear a boutonnière on the left lapel. White carnations are the usual choice for everyone except the groom and his best man, who may wear a white rose, a sprig of stephanotis, or lilies of the valley. Or the groom may have a flower that matches one of those in your bouquet—a subtle touch of sentiment.

Floral Decorations for Ceremony and Reception

Ceremony flowers may vary considerably with the location, the size, and the style of the wedding. In general, elaborate floral decorations are reserved for very large, formal weddings. But a simple chapel sometimes needs more decoration than an ornate cathedral. Discuss what is permitted and what has been done in the past first with the proper authorities of the church. Then ask your florist to visit your wedding site (if he hasn't already) to offer new ideas.

Regardless of the size and mood of your wedding, you'll want to have at least one vase of flowers on each side of the altar. You may also have a number of other arrangements. Imagine delicate sprays of flowers attached to the aisle posts instead of just ribbon bows. These may be placed on every second or third pew, or only on those pews reserved for relatives and special guests. If you're being married in a church with plain windows, you might put an eye-catching arrangement of flowers in each windowsill. When guests are not expected to fill the church, it's nice to have a bank of ferns, palms, or potted flowers to mark the section needed for the ceremony. Ropes of flowers interspersed with ivy or smilax may also be used to partition the church, or they may drape the altar rail.

You may choose any flowers you like, including favorite blossoms too fragile to be used on bouquets. Or have your altar arrangements made of the same flowers carried by the bridesmaids. Even the most attractive home or club needs greens and flowers to form a simple aisle and a decorative background for the ceremony.

Banks of ferns, baskets of cut flowers, or rows of potted plants may partition the room into the appropriate sections. You might place a screen of greens and flowers behind the altar or kneeling bench, or post a *huppah* woven of flowers and greens and add ropes of ribbon intertwined with tiny blossoms to indicate an aisle.

Reception flowers may also be as simple or elaborate as you wish. Carry out your wedding color scheme by repeating the flowers in your bridesmaids' bouquets. Or select something different to harmonize with the surroundings. It's customary to have floral centerpieces on dinner and refreshment tables, and these may be anything from a few sprigs to a long garland of blossoms. You might even choose individual cuttings, small potted plants, or bud vases that guests can take home—for a long time to come, they'll be saying, ''Remember the wedding where. . .''

Be sure that all the arrangements on the bridal table are low enough to not obscure the members of the wedding party. You might place your bridal bouquet in the center of the table, with those of your attendants lined up on either side of it. The cake table is usually decorated with floral sprays or other small arrangements; the cake itself may be topped with flowers, a particularly elegant touch. You may also use floral screens and banks of ferns to form a background for the receiving line. It is a setting that will make guests feel truly welcome.

In a way that everyone can appreciate, flowers symbolize the beauty of the wedding service and a marriage growing in love and devotion.

15
Your Photographs and Publicity

Your marriage ceremony will be over in a few minutes, your reception in a few hours. But your photographs, bridal portrait, wedding candids, and newspaper clippings are keepsakes you'll treasure for years to come. Through them, you and your groom will be able to relive some of your happiest moments and share those precious memories with your family and friends.

Your Bridal Portrait

This is your most important wedding photograph, since it is the one that may be published in the newspaper—displayed in your new home and in those of your relatives. Keep both purposes in mind when you choose your hairstyle, makeup, and

171

background so you'll be as proud of the way your portrait looks twenty years from now as you are when it appears in print.

Most newspapers require that wedding photographs be submitted at least ten days before the scheduled publication date—plan on having your portrait taken about a month before the wedding. If the proper facilities are available, you may arrange to have your portrait done at your bridal salon during the final fitting of your dress. Otherwise, make certain you have your dress delivered in time to go to your photographer's studio. There you can be sure of having the lighting, background, air conditioning, and peaceful surroundings necessary for best results.

Your bridal portrait should look as if it were made on your wedding day, so be sure you carry along all the proper accessories —shoes, petticoat, gloves, jewelry, prayer book. If you wish your flowers to show, give the photographer a detailed description of your bouquet so he can provide an appropriate dummy. Do take his advice on hair and makeup into consideration, but also strive for your own prettiest, most natural look.

Your photographer will take several different shots of you in different poses, then supply proofs of a good selection. You may want to choose one pose for publicity purposes, another for your finished portrait; let the photographer help you decide about which poses will look best in the newspapers (they will be special glossy, black-and-white prints).

Some newspapers will now run portraits of the bride and groom together. If you choose this option, you'll have to make suitable arrangements with your photographer. Your groom, of course, should also plan to wear his full wedding outfit for the picture. Incidentally, since a groom nowadays may even go shopping with the bride for her dress, the old superstition of his not seeing her before the wedding is nothing to worry about.

Your Wedding Candids

The person who photographs your wedding ceremony and reception should be someone with the knowledge and experience to get the kind of pictures you'll display with pride. After all, you won't be able to repeat the whole day "once more for the cameras"! A photographer specializing in weddings is most reliable. This doesn't mean that your friends should be discouraged from bringing their cameras to the wedding. Let them shoot all the pictures they want. As long as they don't have the complete responsibility, it won't matter if they get caught up in the festivities and forget all about snapping your grandmother with your father, or about taking the classic receiving line photo.

It is nice to include posed photographs in your wedding album to make sure no important people are missed. But the pictures that may be the most talked about long after are those that catch spontaneous action (the flower girl waltzing with her brother, a happy maid kicking her shoe off) and unconscious facial expressions—true "candid" shots.

Whatever you do, don't make your guests wait around while you and other members of your wedding party pose for the camera. Plan in advance to have your posed shots taken as quickly and unobtrusively as possible. If you want to be photographed with your parents or your bridesmaids, for example, allow time for these pictures to be done at home as soon as you finish dressing. Since the bridal party leaves the church before any of the guests, you should arrive at the reception in time to pose for several pictures before the first guests appear. A formal shot of you and your groom might also be taken at that time. The ushers and best man can be photographed after the receiving line forms.

Although a competent photographer doesn't need coaching to capture the highlights of a wedding, he does need to know your personal plans and wishes and the names of any people you don't want him to leave out. You should make sure that he's familiar with any regulations or preferences of the clergy, too. Some churches, for example, do not allow flashbulbs or altar photographs during the ceremony. This may apply particularly if you're thinking of having movies or videotapes of your wedding made. Check with your minister, priest, or rabbi, then be certain the photographer knows how to preserve the solemnity and dignity of your wedding ceremony.

Gifts of Photographs

Customarily the bride's family covers the cost of the wedding album, and it remains with the couple. The couple should also have a picture of each other to put on a desk or dresser at home or at work. However, having prints made for both sets of parents is a thoughtful gesture. At the very least, the groom's parents should receive six pictures: possibly a small-size portrait of the bride, the couple, all the members of their immediate family together with the newlyweds, both sets of parents together, the receiving line, the parents' table. These prints may or may not be bound into a miniature album or encased in suitable frames. It is not necessary to show the groom's family proofs, but this does give them the opportunity of saying, "Now that's our son. Could you tell us how we can order half a dozen for ourselves?"

Each attendant would certainly appreciate a small print of the whole wedding party, with the bride and groom. And the guests? Having someone on hand at the reception with an instant camera and plenty of film is one way you can honor them with a memory of being there.

Pre-Wedding Publicity

In large metropolitan areas, the only advance publicity a marriage receives is the engagement announcement (see Chapter 1 for suggested wording). In many smaller communities, however, the activities surrounding an upcoming wedding make society-page news for weeks before the ceremony. Some papers report the details of showers and other parties given in honor of the bride and groom; others publish the wedding plans a week or two in advance. Such an item might read:

Plans for the marriage of Miss Cynthia Joy Dumbrowski, daughter of Mr. and Mrs. Frederick Hugh Dumbrowski of Briarcliff Drive, and Mr. Ronald Lloyd Felker, Jr., son of Mrs. Ronald Lloyd Felker and the late Mr. Felker of Omaha, Nebraska, were announced today by the bride. The ceremony will be performed at the First Presbyterian Church of Lockport, with the Reverend Roland Saunders officiating.

Miss Dumbrowski will be attended by her sister, Mrs. Kevin McGovern of Lexington, Kentucky, matron of honor. The bridesmaids will be Miss Jessica Kramer of Baton Rouge, Louisiana, Miss Donna Calabrese, Miss Andrea Gould, and Mrs. Kenneth Bronson of Lockport. Miss Leslie McGovern, the bride's niece, will be flower girl. Dennis O'Connor of Omaha will be Mr. Felker's best man. Kevin McGovern, William Harris, and Stanley Janski of Omaha, and William Hertz of Lockport will serve as ushers.

The ceremony will be followed by a reception at the White Hills Lodge.

Before submitting an item of this type, study your newspaper carefully to make sure it considers such information newsworthy, then follow the form usually used for such stories as closely as possible.

Your Wedding Announcement

It's customary to publish the details of a formal wedding in the couple's hometown newspapers. A morning wedding is sometimes written up in an evening paper the same day, but most wedding stories are published the day after the ceremony. Check with your newspaper in advance to learn its exact requirements and deadlines. Some, for example, require the bride to fill out a standard form and submit it to the society editor ten days or more before the wedding. Others want telephoned confirmation that the wedding has actually taken place before they will go ahead and publish the story. Occasionally, they will ask you to pay a fee.

If your paper does not supply wedding announcement forms, type the information double-spaced on one side of plain white 8½-x-11-inch paper. Be sure to include your name, address, and telephone number (or those of someone in your community who can be called for verification and additional details) in the upper right-hand corner, just as you did with your engagement announcement. The date you'd like the announcement published should appear as well.

If you send a photograph with your wedding story, it should be a 5-x-7-inch or 8-x-10-inch glossy black-and-white print of your bridal portrait. Tape a typed line of identification to the photo in case it gets separated from the story. Enclose the picture, announcement, and a piece of stiff cardboard in a manila envelope and address it to the society-page editor—mail it or drop it off. If you send photographs to more than one paper in the same city, you may want to submit different poses to each.

A typical wedding announcement reads:

Miss Patricia Clark Butler, daughter of Mr. and Mrs. Clifford Marion Butler of South Orange, was married this afternoon to Mr. Lewis Herbert Sullivan, son of Mr. and Mrs. Howard Mitchell Sullivan of Short Hills. Msgr. Patrick Flynn of Englewood, uncle of the bride, performed the ceremony in Trinity Church in South Orange.

The bride, escorted by her father, wore an ivory dress of organza trimmed with Venise lace. Bands of matching lace edged her chapel train and veil. She carried a cascade of white roses and stephanotis.

Miss Carla Butler, sister of the bride, was maid of honor. Bridesmaids were Misses Gloria Geller and Linda Kerr of

South Orange, Mrs. Gino DeGeorgio of Teaneck, and Mrs. Francis Demery of Buffalo, New York.

Arthur Clay of Newark served as best man. The ushers were Neil Butler, brother of the bride, Nathan Freeman of Short Hills, and Harvey Lyons and David Chan of New York.

Some newspapers also publish descriptions of the bridesmaids' and mothers' dresses and flowers, the location of the reception, details of the newlyweds' respective educational backgrounds, professional affiliations, grandparents' names, honeymoon plans, and other information. (For example, if you will continue to use your maiden name after marriage, you could include a sentence mentioning this.) Use published stories in your newspaper as a guide to how much or how little to include.

Small weddings and second marriages—happily—can be announced, although the stories may not go into detail, covering only the basic facts shown in the first paragraph above. A prior marriage is sometimes mentioned in a line saying, "The bride's previous marriage ended in divorce."

If your parents are divorced, the announcement would read, ". . .the daughter of Mrs. Clark Butler of South Orange and Mr. Clifford Marion Butler of Newark." If one of your parents is widowed, the standard phrasing is ". . .the daughter of Mrs. Clifford Marion Butler and the late Mr. Butler." If your mother has remarried and you have been adopted by your stepfather, that information appears later in the story, perhaps reporting that your stepfather gave you away. Is it your groom's parents who are divorced? The usual wording can easily be adapted.

However and wherever people hear of your wedding, it is the best of news.

16
Wedding Gifts

The gifts you receive as a bride not only provide many of the basic needs for your new home, they are wonderful tokens of friendship as well. Only those persons who accept invitations to your reception are obligated to send gifts, but you also may receive presents from others who wanted very much to attend but couldn't. You'll receive packages from people you don't even know since it is customary for all gifts given before the wedding —including those from relatives and friends of the groom—to be sent to the bride.

Your fiancé, your mother, your honor attendant, and your bridesmaids may all join in the fun and help you open your gifts. Just be careful not to lose any enclosure cards. And keep accurate records of who sent what to avoid mixing up gifts or forgetting thank-you notes. If you haven't already gotten a wedding planning notebook with a section for gifts, request or buy a gift-record book from your stationer, bridal salon, or wedding gift registry consultant at your favorite store.

As you open each package, list the gift immediately in your book, adding an identifying description of the item, the name and address of the donor, the store from which it came (in case you want to exchange it later), the date it arrived, and the date on which you mail your thank-you note. If you expect a lot of gifts, number your list and stick a corresponding number to each item. Then you won't confuse the silver candy dish from your great-aunt with the one from your groom's boss. Some gifts and wedding books include self-adhesive numbers for this purpose. You may want to recruit your honor attendant's help with the gift record.

Registering for Gifts

Listing your preferences at your store's wedding gift registry is becoming a bridal tradition, and it will be a real pleasure for you and your groom to make your choices together. Registering is also a courtesy to guests—you spare them the time and effort of hunting for the perfect gift for you, as well as the possible disappointment of buying you something you don't love or can't use.

As the bride, you should be careful to list items that suit the budgets of all your guests, as well as the many gift-giving occasions they will attend for you. An oven thermometer a graduate student could bring to a shower will mean as much as the silver coffee service your grandparents send before your wedding.

How do you let people know where you're registered politely? A shower host or hostess can note the store name on invitations. Your mother, his mother, and your attendants might also spread the word. Whenever someone asks what you would like for your wedding, you yourself can answer, "John and I are registered at Addington's. You might find something you like as much as we do there." Many people, of course, genuinely enjoy choosing gifts themselves, perhaps wrapping them prettily, and this will always be their privilege as gift-givers. And while a few newspapers will accept a line such as, "The couple have registered at Addington's," to print along with the engagement announcement, do check with the society editor or office of the publisher before sending in this information.

Your Thank-You Notes

Start writing your thank-you notes as soon as you receive your first wedding gifts. You must send a personal, handwritten letter of appreciation for each gift you receive, even one from a close friend you've thanked in person and see every day at work. The only exceptions to this thanks-in-writing rule are gifts from your fiancé and from your parents, although they, too, might treasure a special letter from you. (Imagine your parents reading again and again together your words of appreciation for the gift of money toward that down payment on a house.)

Thank-you notes need not be long, but they should be prompt. In general, you should try to acknowledge gifts that arrive before your wedding within two weeks of their arrival. Those coming later should be acknowledged within a month after your honeymoon. If you expect to receive more gifts than you could possibly acknowledge within this time, you may send printed cards to let your friends know their gifts arrived safely. These cards, which must be followed by personal notes as soon as possible, read:

Miss Ann Marie Brown
acknowledges with thanks
the receipt of your wedding gift
and will take pleasure in writing a personal note
at an early date

The classic thank-you note is written in blue or black ink on a good grade of folded notepaper in ivory or white. Your name or monogram may be printed or embossed on the notes if you wish, but you won't use your married name or initial until after the wedding. Colored, decorated notes also may be chosen—the most important thing is to make certain a thank-you is sent.

A thank-you note to a married couple is traditionally addressed to the wife, with her husband referred to in the body of the note. Nowadays, you may address both if you prefer. Do mention your own fiancé or husband whenever possible. For example, "Dear Mrs. Clark, John and I are delighted with the beautiful vase we received today from you and Mr. Clark. . . ."

You may sign notes to relatives and close friends with your first name only, but use your full name to people you don't know as well. After the wedding, you may include your maiden name whenever necessary for identification. For example, you may sign yourself, "Ann Smith" or "Ann Brown Smith," but never "Mrs. John Smith." If you plan to continue using your maiden name, you might take this chance to notify your friends by signing your notes "Ann Brown" after the wedding.

It's much easier to see that your thank-you notes sound sincere and spontaneous if you set aside time to write a few every day. When trying to write several dozen at once, you will find it difficult to make them all as enthusiastic as you—and the gift-givers —would like.

Each letter should be as warm and personal as possible. Everyone loves exuberant praise for something chosen with care and affection. Describe the gift itself and how you plan to use it. If it's one of those inevitable "mystery gifts" with an obscure purpose, refer to it by color or material. It's much better to say thanks for a specific "blue glass piece" or "silver container" than for a vague "lovely gift." Try to put at least one thought besides "thank you" into each note. You might include an invitation to visit, a comment about the wedding, or a word or two about your new apartment—some personal touch. Many couples find gifts of money difficult to acknowledge, but they can be easy if you just mention how you plan to use the money. The following would be appropriate for a gift check:

Dear Uncle Ed,

Thank you so much for the generous wedding check. It was a wonderful surprise. John and I have added it to savings earmarked for a car—and thanks to you, we're almost there. We'll be driving around to see you soon!

Love,
Ann

A situation, again, that often perplexes the bride is when she unwraps a gift she can't identify—and months after the wedding at that. The idea is not to worry about your confusion but take advantage of it:

Dear Miss Martin,

Thank you for the beautifully engraved silver piece—it was such a nice surprise to find it waiting when John and I came home from work. There is a reason I've remembered you as someone who could always brighten a routine day. It felt like Christmas all over. Thank you again.

Sincerely,
Ann Brown Smith

If you haven't met the gift-givers yet—they are friends of your fiancé's family, perhaps—suggest a time when you might:

Dear Mrs. Robbins:

Thank you very much for the blender you and Mr. Robbins sent. Both John and his brother Larry tell me you serve some of the thickest milkshakes in town. Now we can too! I can't wait to meet you at the wedding. Again, many thanks.

Sincerely yours,
Ann Brown

When you receive a single gift from several relatives, bridesmaids, or friends, you should write each one a separate note. However, if the gift came from a large group—your co-workers, for example—one thank-you note addressed to the group is sufficient (be sure to thank everyone in person as well):

Dear Co-Workers,

Thank you, thank you for the place setting of china. Now John and I have service for twelve—just the right number to host the annual partners' dinner. How did you ever guess? Seriously, we do appreciate it—and I can't wait to get back with our honeymoon snapshots for you to see.

With much affection,
Ann Smith

What do you do when you really don't care for the gift and you can't return it? Find something nice to say about it or the person who sent it, for his or her feelings are undoubtedly very important to you.

Dear Bob and Jan,

Thanks so much for the lamp that's a gum machine too! Ann and I haven't stopped talking about it—and it's sure to be a conversation piece whenever we have people over. You two are always so clever and so much fun, we intend you to be among our first guests. Thanks again,

Best,
John

Although the responsibility for acknowledging all gifts—received before, at, or after the wedding—has traditionally belonged to the bride, your groom can write thank-you notes as well, either for gifts given at parties he has attended or for those that have come with his name on them as well as yours, especially if they are from people he knows best. After all, you will be enjoying your gifts together.

Displaying Your Gifts

Nearly everyone likes to admire wedding presents, especially when the gift he or she has given holds a place of honor. Some guests even wait until they've had a chance to look at the gift display before selecting a wedding present.

See that your display is set up in a room that is not in constant use, arranging your gifts on rows of card tables covered with white tablecloths or sheets. You may start your display as soon as you have six or eight gifts, adding more as they arrive. Group gifts into categories, with silver on one table, glassware on another, electrical appliances on a third, and so on. Display only token place settings of dinnerware, flatware, and glassware. Scatter similar gifts so that it's not obvious to viewers that you've received twelve sets of salt and pepper shakers. If you file the gift cards elsewhere, you can display just one set of exact duplicates, and each donor will think you've received only his. Do not put out gifts of money, or place modest gifts immediately next to very generous ones. Garlands of greens, small bowls of flowers, or clusters of ribbon from the packages make your array more festive.

It's wise to take out a temporary floater policy insuring your gifts while they are on display. You may also want to ask a neighbor to keep an eye on the house during the ceremony or other times when the house will be empty.

Incidentally, gifts sent before the wedding are likely to arrive at the R.S.V.P. address indicated on the wedding invitation. This means the bride who will travel to her parents' hometown for the wedding may be counting on her mother to collect and display gifts. If so, you will certainly need to make special arrangements to transport the gifts to wherever you and your groom will be living.

If your reception is held at home, guests will see the gift display then. But you may ask friends to come by and see the gifts or give a special luncheon, tea, or bridesmaids' party to show your presents. You might leave your gift display up for a week after the ceremony so friends and relatives can drop by to see it. With the letdown that comes after a major event in life, and with you off on your honeymoon, your parents might welcome the company.

Expecting gifts at the reception? You may carry a pretty white purse to collect envelopes containing money and checks, if this is the custom among your family and friends. But even if you do, envelopes should then be entrusted to an usher or close family member. (Endorse them when you change to your honeymoon travel clothes, and this person can also deposit them in a bank account while you are away.) Packages might warrant a guard at a particularly busy public hall or restaurant. In either case, it is safest not to open and display these gifts at the reception—you don't want anyone's carefully chosen present to you to get lost!

Damaged Gifts

When you receive a damaged gift from a local store, return it for replacement. If it came from an out-of-town shop, write a letter of explanation and wait for instructions. Be sure to ask them not to tell the purchaser of the damage. More than one bride has neglected to make such a request, only to learn that the store did call the person—long after she'd sent a thank-you note making no mention of the problem.

If a broken gift was mailed by the purchaser, check the wrappings for an insurance stamp. It is there? Then return the package with a note of explanation so that he or she can collect the insurance and make a replacement. If the gift was not insured, however, don't mention the damage as it may make the person feel obligated to send another gift. Damaged gifts are not displayed unless they can be arranged so that the crack, dent, etc. doesn't show.

Exchanging Gifts

No matter how careful you and your fiancé are about registering your gift preferences, you're bound to receive a few gifts
you can't use. Some duplicates, especially of breakable items and
of things you can always use more of (towels, blankets) are nice
to have, but it is practical to exchange gifts you really don't need
—as long as it can be done without the giver knowing. Never ask
where a gift was purchased so that you can exchange it, and don't
mention duplication or exchange in your thank-you note.

Returning Gifts

When a wedding is merely postponed, you send an announcement to all the guests, and keep the presents you've already received. (See Chapter 5.) When a wedding is cancelled, however,
every gift—even those that have been monogrammed—must go
back to the person who sent it. A note expressing gratitude and
explaining that the wedding will not take place accompanies each
present, but you need give no reason for the cancellation.

Monogramming

There was a time when almost every wedding gift—from silver
to linens—bore a monogram. Today, however, most brides who
want something monogrammed have it done after the wedding.
You might even ask the consultant at the wedding gift registry to
indicate your wishes on your preference list. That way you can
avoid the "no exchange" rule that usually applies to monogrammed items and make sure your monograms will read exactly
as you want them to (for example, if you are keeping your maiden

name after marriage or designing a contemporary monogram that includes both your husband's and your first initials).

A monogram is a personal trademark that should be chosen with care. The most common style for silver flatware is a single initial engraved on the handles. Triple-initial monograms, in a variety of styles, are also popular. The bride's first, maiden, and married initials are the traditional choice, but you may also use your first initial, your husband's, and your married surname in the center. If your initials spell a word like *BAD* or *JAR,* think about a monogram in which the last initial is in the center and larger than the other two: *bDa* or *jRa.*

Gifts for Attendants

It's customary to give each of your attendants a small gift as a token of appreciation and as a memento of the occasion. These need not be expensive, but should be relatively permanent items of a personal nature. Each bridesmaid gets an identical gift, but honor attendants usually receive something a little more special. The same is true for your groom's ushers and his best man. Gifts to your attendants are distributed before the wedding, often at the bridesmaids' luncheon and bachelor party or, if preferred, at the rehearsal dinner.

You may give your attendants almost anything you think they'd like, but the usual choice is something that can be worn in the wedding or that can be monogrammed and engraved with the wedding date. In the first category are gloves, pearls, or earrings for the bridesmaids (or their dresses, if you wish to relieve them of that expense); studs, cuff links, tie bars, or stickpins for the ushers. Women's gifts that monogram nicely include bracelets, pins, pendants, and silver hair combs. For men, it's money clips, belt buckles, key rings, or pewter mugs. Or you may break with tradition and give each attendant a gift chosen especially for her or for him—from a sewing basket to a series of theater tickets to a special golf club.

Gifts to Each Other

There is nothing that says you and your groom must exchange gifts, but most couples do. They choose something they know will be treasured for years—for its usefulness as well as for its sentimental value. For example, you might give your groom a good watch, a pair of gold cuff links, a piece of luggage, or a handsome wallet. He might surprise you with a watch, too, or with fine jewelry, an attaché case, or a frame of sterling silver to hold his picture. Engraving or embossing the gift with initials, wedding date, and perhaps a few very personal words will remind you both of your special feelings for one another, and the deep commitment you have made to share the years ahead.

Anniversary Gifts

Picturing the years ahead, you may find yourself thinking of anniversary gifts. Today, when couples work hard to make marriage last and regard each additional year together as the best reason to celebrate, gifts become a natural and lovely way to mark the happy occasion. From time to time, the festivities will resemble a "second" wedding reception, with vows renewed, family and friends on hand, champagne toasts. At the thirtieth or fiftieth, for instance, there could be a receiving line including adult children. Other years the couple might enjoy a romantic—and most private—candlelight dinner at a restaurant. In any event, a store's wedding gift registry will often keep a list of gift preferences up to date to remind anniversary party guests (not to mention a forgetful husband or wife!) what the couple would still appreciate. The following are the traditional anniversary gifts.

1st:	paper	*13th:*	lace
2nd:	cotton	*14th:*	ivory
3rd:	leather	*15th:*	crystal
4th:	linen	*20th:*	china
5th:	wood	*25th:*	silver
6th:	iron	*30th:*	pearls
7th:	wool	*35th:*	coral, jade
8th:	bronze	*40th:*	rubies
9th:	pottery	*45th:*	sapphires
10th:	tin, aluminum	*50th:*	gold
11th:	steel	*55th:*	emeralds
12th:	silk	*60th:*	diamonds

When giving anniversary presents, use your imagination. Paper on the first could mean anything from magazine subscriptions to stock certificates; silver on the twenty-fifth, a silver ice bucket or plane tickets west to the land of the silver screen. Feel free to interpret the traditional suggestions in a contemporary way as well. Luggage on the third anniversary could easily be vinyl; candlesticks on the fifteenth, glass that's crystal-clear. What if the husband wants a clock on the first anniversary to keep time through the coming years, and the wife a diamond to add to her ring? The most-wanted gift is always the best gift. Incidentally, couples celebrating anniversaries may also treat others to gifts, in appreciation of their continued friendship.

Whether for wedding or anniversary, gifts make memories. Through the years, you will look at them, touch them again and again. And each will remind you that there always have been people around you who want all that is good for you and for your marriage.

17
Wedding Guests

A wedding guest's chief function is to wish the bride and groom well. But there is, nowadays, a large variety of wedding styles. Depending on what the couple choose, you might receive an invitation to a very formal service and seated dinner at eight or a surfside ceremony at dawn. Each wedding style suggests an appropriate response, gift, and dress—a way, if you will, of letting the couple know you share their happiness.

Receiving a Wedding Invitation

A formal, traditional invitation to a wedding ceremony and reception must always be acknowledged promptly. Answering in writing is most courteous, as this helps the wedding hosts keep track of replies.

A reply to a formal invitation is written on plain white or cream-colored notepaper in blue, blue-black, or black ink. A formal acceptance reads:

> Mr. and Mrs. Joel Kagyama
> accept with pleasure
> the invitation of
> Mr. and Mrs. Ernest Carr Burke
> for Saturday, the fourth of April
> at half after four o'clock

It is not necessary to repeat the name of the bride and groom, but including the date and time indicates that these have been correctly understood. Including the location is optional. Wording and spacing should duplicate that of the invitation.

A formal regret is usually worded:

> Mr. Jean-Jacques De Lille
> regrets that he is unable to accept
> the kind invitation of
> Mr. and Mrs. Ernest Carr Burke
> for Saturday, the fourth of April

A regret does not repeat the time or the place, merely the date. No reason need be given but you may, if you like, enclose a separate personal note to explain why you cannot attend and to wish the bride and groom a life full of all good things.

A note is nice for an informal, handwritten invitation or one that is of a contemporary, personalized design. You can use your favorite stationery. For example:

Dear Stephanie,

Rick and I are delighted to be included among the guests at Rochelle's wedding on the fifteenth of June at Central Methodist Church. We are looking forward to both the ceremony and the reception.

Affectionately,
Becky

An informal note of regret might read:

Dear Stephanie,
   Charlotte and I regret that we will be away on the fif-teenth of June as my younger sister will be graduating that day. If we hadn't already made plans, you know nothing could keep us from Shelly's wedding.
   Please give Shelly and Norman our best wishes for their future   happiness.   *Fondly,*
                                                       Gary

If a response card is included with the invitation, use that for your reply. You may slip it into a separate note should you wish to add a more personal message.

When considering an invitation, you can assume that children and others who may be living with you are invited only if their names appear on the inside envelope. If the hosts address the invitation "Miss Marx," then they expect this woman to attend the wedding—not the mother who may be sharing her house. If your children are invited, take them only if you'll be able to keep a close watch over them during the ceremony and reception. Otherwise, arrange to leave them home. Incidentally, parents who are unable to get out as often as they like find a wedding is the perfect excuse to indulge in a much-needed date. Single guests should not bring a special man or woman friend along unless specifically asked—remember, a reception is a wonderful occasion to meet new   people.

Weddings Out of Town

Is the wedding out of town? At the time you accept the invitation, you may request a map or other written directions to the wedding site from the bride's or groom's family. There will be nothing more disappointing to you and to them than your missing the ceremony because you were driving along every highway and byway in the area searching for the church. It won't hurt either to double-check the instructions you receive with someone else—perhaps the local police.

Some families of the bride and groom may recommend hotels to out-of-town guests, sightseeing ideas and such. But if they don't, try to take care of these details on your own—families will appreciate being left free to deal with last-minute planning. In this case, you are also expected to cover costs of accommodations and meals yourself. Should a friend or relative entertain you, at a breakfast the day of the wedding, for example, do send a thank-you note.

Receiving a Wedding Announcement

A wedding announcement does not obligate you in any way: Neither a gift nor a personal acknowledgment is necessary. When dear friends are involved, however, it is a thoughtful gesture to send a personal note of good wishes to the couple, and perhaps, to their parents as well. Feel like giving a gift? Do!

Sending a Wedding Gift

Always plan on sending a gift when you accept a reception invitation. In the rare event you are invited to a wedding ceremony alone (if, for example, an illness in the couple's immediate families means a reception would be inappropriate, or if a group invitation has been extended to members of the church congregation), a gift is not required. Nor is it when a reception invitation has been declined. Attending the second wedding of the bride or the groom when you went to the first long ago? Traditionally no gift need be given, but a token of your happy feelings would certainly be appreciated. Of course, your gift choice this time will be somewhat different. Rather than flatware, a serving piece, perhaps; or instead of a complete place setting of crystal, two toasting glasses and a bottle of quality champagne. If, too, you cannot attend a reception but want to give a gift—feel free.

A wedding gift should be sent to the bride at her home or at the R.S.V.P. address. It may be mailed or sent directly from the store. It's customary to enclose a gift card with a personal note handwritten on it. Gifts sent after the wedding are addressed to the bride and groom wherever they are living.

A wedding gift should be chosen with careful thought and an eye to practicality. It need not be expensive; sometimes a modest gift selected with imagination and affection pleases the couple most of all. If you are unfamiliar with their taste, it is best to play it safe with a classic item that can be used in many ways—a Revere bowl, for example, can hold anything from mashed potatoes to mail to a bouquet of flowers. The easiest way to please the couple, of course, is to choose something from their list at the wedding gift registry. Don't know the store? Telephone the bride's or groom's mother, maid or matron of honor, or couple themselves.

Money also makes a suitable, and always appreciated, wedding gift. Checks sent before the wedding are made out to the bride; those given on wedding day or later, to the couple.

While packages are brought to the reception in many locales, seeing to it the gift gets to the appropriate home address beforehand is not only traditional but wise. That way, the couple can assure safe storage of the gift you've gone to the trouble and expense to provide, as well as make efficient arrangements to move it to the place they'll be living.

Should you have sent your gift rather than deliver it in person, you can expect a thank-you note from the bride (or from the groom, nowadays). If, however, several months have passed since the wedding and still no word, it is understandable that you would be concerned about the gift's safe arrival. You may phone to make certain the store from which you had the gift sent actually delivered it. Or have the post office trace your package—keeping insurance receipts for all wedding gifts you mail does make sense. If the gift seems to have been lost or damaged, you may replace it, enclosing a note to the couple. If all appears in order, it's up to you whether you ask them about the present. You may find it difficult to check without implying their manners are amiss. A casual remark made during conversation the next time you see them (or their parents, perhaps) is most likely to be received in the spirit it's given. "How's that warming tray working out?" for example, may bring you exactly the reassurance you need—that the couple not only got it but used it at their first dinner party, and it was a big help.

Dressing for the Wedding

Wedding guests dress as they would for almost any other social event of the same hour and season. Men usually wear suits; women, street-length outfits in any color except all-black or all-white (black is the custom for funerals, white detracts from the special role reserved for the bride). When in doubt, check with the bride's mother or groom's mother: "Esther, what are you planning to wear to Wendy's wedding? I'm getting the whole family's outfits together, and we'll take our cues from you." The bride's mother may advise guests on whether pants outfits or bare-shoulder looks are appropriate for the church. Guests may wear formal attire to large formal weddings in the evening.

Church Wedding Procedures

Guests without pew cards should arrive at the site of the ceremony thirty minutes before the appointed time, even earlier for a very large gathering. People with reserved seats should arrive about twenty minutes before the ceremony. Guests getting there later than ten minutes before the ceremony should seat themselves quietly or else remain in the rear of the church during the ceremony.

When they arrive at the church, guests are met in the vestibule by an usher who generally asks whether they are friends of the bride or the groom. The right side of the altar is for the groom's relatives and friends, the left side for the bride's, in Christian weddings. (The reverse is true for many Jewish weddings.) A friend of both bride and groom says so and is seated in the best available spot. A woman guest takes the usher's right arm and is escorted down the aisle to her seat. Her male escort walks a few steps behind them. Sometimes the usher will simply lead the way, so a couple can walk together. Or he will let you know that both sides are sitting together—do as he says. It is customary for guests and ushers to carry on polite conversation in low tones as they proceed down the aisle. Quiet talk with other guests is also all right until the wedding procession begins.

It is not necessary for guests to carry out unfamiliar rituals, especially if their own faith would leave them uncomfortable doing so. But it is polite to follow the lead of the families seated in the front pews. Generally guests of another faith are expected to stand when the families stand, but may remain seated rather than kneel.

When it comes to gestures in a personalized ceremony the couple have asked the guests to make—congregational hymn singing, exchanging handclasps and a brief message with the individuals next to them—honor the request even if you don't quite understand it. When you found the touch meaningful, by all means say so; otherwise withhold comment at least until the wedding day is past.

After the recessional, guests remain in their seats until the ushers have escorted the families of the bride and groom, including the grandmothers and other close relatives, out of the church. Frequently the ushers will indicate the time to leave by returning to stand at the side of the pew, signaling guests to file out row by row. Incidentally, should you need directions to the reception site, rest rooms, and so on, the ushers are the people to ask.

At the Reception

All reception guests pass along the receiving line, greeting and shaking hands with everyone. A guest who doesn't know the bride's mother introduces himself so she can pass his name down the line: "Hi, Mrs. Atkins. I'm Indiri Shakib, Glenda's old friend from music camp. I really did enjoy the violin solo." It's customary to make some remark about the wedding, the bride, or the newly married couple, depending on how well you know the persons involved. It's traditional to congratulate the groom and to wish the bride happiness. Considerate guests move quickly down the line so that others are not kept waiting behind them. Women wearing gloves can keep them on in the receiving line.

Once past the line, guests go directly to the area where refreshments are served. (If the receiving line has been held in the church vestibule or on the church steps, this means the ushers will point the guests on to the reception site.) If the reception is to be a seated luncheon or dinner, they should seek their reserved places, or choose a seat at one of the unreserved tables. At a tea or cocktail reception, guests may serve themselves and circulate, introducing themselves to one another whenever necessary. The wedding party take their places at the bridal table and the traditional toasts are proposed. Every guest should drink every toast—whether his beverage preference is champagne, iced tea, or ginger ale. After the toasts, the meal is served or the bride and groom cut the cake. At a tea or cocktail reception, the festivities may begin long before the cake is cut. And at a very large reception, the father of the bride may see to it that dancing is well underway before the couple appear on the scene for their traditional dance with each other and with their parents.

Wedding receptions have no specified length, but the party usually continues as long as the bride and groom remain. Once they have made their going-away dash through a shower of rice or rose petals, however, guests may take their leave. They find a member of the bride's immediate family, if possible, and say something like, "Thanks for a really enjoyable evening, Mrs. Atkins. It was a beautiful wedding, I'm sure you must be proud of Glenda." The host and hostess are inundated with farewells? Phone or write the next day with, "I had a wonderful time!"

18
Going Away

The reception should be great fun—and you and your groom can stay as long as you wish the party to go on. Being the guests of honor, you are traditionally the first to leave, and people may take their cues from you. There is no reason, of course, that your family and friends cannot continue to dance and dine and drink if your parents (or other wedding hosts) are on hand and eager for them to do so. In this case, making your departure while the festivities are in full swing may give you that elated feeling that comes from knowing things are going even better than you hoped. Staying till the end? Make sure guests feel free to go.

Saying Good-bye

When you are ready to leave, simply pass the word to your bridesmaids and other single friends to prepare to catch your bouquet; and, if you wish, to the groomsmen and single men that the garter will be tossed. Once the laughter and excitement have died down, you and your groom can slip away to change.

Your honor attendant goes with you to help, and the best man accompanies the groom. Both of you should make sure your going-away outfits are comfortable and suitable to your method of transportation. Will you be taking a trip in your car cross-country? Good-looking pants and tops for you both, with a sweater or jacket in case it gets cool makes sense. If you'll be off on a cruise, a sporty dress for you; a blazer and trousers for him may be best. Also consider where you'll be staying that first night. You may want to arrive in a wrinkle-free suit and heels at a city hotel; at a small-town inn, in separates. The classic accessory for a woman on this special occasion is a flower corsage to complement her outfit. A casual look might call for flowers in the hair. Sometimes these flowers will be part of the bride's bouquet, and detached from it before it is tossed to the single women.

When you are both dressed, your honor attendant should notify your parents so they can come to say good-bye in private. This is apt to be a sensitive time for them. Let your parents know how much you appreciate everything they've done: "Mom, everyone was saying how good the food was, thanks for your help with the menu. Dad, I'm glad you thought to get insurance for all those gifts, you've always looked out for me pretty well." When your groom has finished telling his own parents good-bye, he will come for you and thank your parents. Your honor attendants, incidentally, can see that your wedding clothes are returned to wherever you wish after the reception's all over.

You may be tempted to leave the reception quietly through the back door, but your guests will never forgive you if you try to sneak away. Supplies of rice, or birdseed, will be handed around to the guests while you are changing. (Paper confetti and flower petals are sometimes used, but hard to clean up and easy to slip on.) Young friends or brothers and sisters will love carrying out this assignment.

Most couples hold hands and run under that shower of good wishes from their friends, but peddling off on bicycles or climbing into a horse-drawn carriage are other means of reaching the getaway car. The best man will have taken care of putting the luggage in the car and keeping practical jokers away—it is his responsibility, too, to see that any decorations that might block the driver's vision or hamper hearing are removed.

En Route

Traveling by plane, you should allow plenty of time in the airport before your flight, and of course, be patient in line and courteous to fellow passengers. If you have an inside seat on the airplane, try to get up only when you absolutely must. It isn't necessary to tip flight attendants, but do thank them when you file out. Should your flight be delayed or cancelled, resulting in problems with connections, or should your luggage stray (pack all essentials like prescriptions in a carry-on bag just in case), ask to see a "special service representative." Tip skycaps for each bag they carry.

On overnight train trips, tip the porter every night for making up your berth and for giving you a wake-up call in the morning. There are also a few conventions to observe on board a commercial ship. Except for captains and doctors with professional titles, all personnel are addressed as "Mr." (or "Miss, Mrs., or Ms."). Finding out as soon as possible where you will be seated for dinner is customary as well. You may request table changes, but if you do, make it within two days after arrival and tip the steward for the changes arranged.

At Your Destination

At your hotel, your groom may sign the register for you both, although many hotels nowadays ask for the first names of the husband and the wife ("Mrs. Shirley Moore and Mr. Russell

Moore"). Don't be afraid to say you're newlyweds! You may be surprised with complimentary flowers, fruit, or champagne. Bellhops should, of course, be tipped for carrying suitcases to the room. Any problems with the room should be directed to the assistant manager or manager at the desk. If you really do not wish to be disturbed, it is essential that you hang the "Do Not Disturb" sign on the doorknob; otherwise, the staff may knock or even walk in earlier than you'd like. During your stay, leave a tip each day for the person who straightens up—perhaps on the pillow. Because staff assignments may rotate daily, waiting until the end of your visit to tip in a lump sum means the appropriate people may not be remembered. A call ahead to the desk will assure that your bill is ready when you check out.

In foreign countries, mastering the native words for "please" and "thank you" can help with service. Any tips you give should always be in the local currency; restaurants, of course, may include the gratuities in the bill—ask. The passport you applied for before your wedding will have been issued in your maiden name. Taking a copy of your marriage certificate on your travels may, in this case, be wise. With evidence, you can visit the local American embassy and have your passport adjusted to indicate your new marital status if necessary.

As soon as you reach your destination, it's nice to phone or telegram your groom's parents and your own to let them know you arrived safely and to thank them again for the wedding. Many couples also enjoy shopping for souvenirs to bring the people "back home." A special gift for those at work who lived through the trials and tribulations of planning—"The caterer just called and said he couldn't get pink tablecloths!" "I can't believe it, my mother finally found her dress!" is sure to be appreciated.

Your Home Together

When does the groom carry the bride over the threshold? After the honeymoon, at the apartment or house where they will make their home. This is one of the few very private traditions surrounding marriage, and a moment not to be missed.

When you begin summing up your memories, you'll both realize that your own wedding has a special beauty and meaning for you no other ceremony will ever match. Whether it's a simple family service or an elaborate celebration before hundreds, your wedding will always have a place in your heart. It is, after all, the beginning of your married life together. May it be a long, prosperous, and increasingly happy one.

Index